WIRRAL
Tragic Tales

*For all those who have fallen victim to
loss and tragedy*

WIRRAL
Tragic Tales

Daniel K. Longman

Foreword by Tom Slemen

First published in the United Kingdom in 2007 by
Sutton Publishing

Reprinted in 2009 by
The History Press
The Mill, Brimscombe Port,
Stroud, Gloucestershire, GL5 2QG
www.thehistorypress.co.uk

Reprinted 2011, 2012

Copyright © Daniel K. Longman, 2011

All rights reserved. No part of this publication may be reproduced, stored in a retrieval system, or transmitted, in any form or by any means, electronic, mechanical, photocopying, recording or otherwise, without the prior permission of the publisher and copyright holder.

Daniel K. Longman has asserted the moral right to be identified as the author of this work.

British Library Cataloguing in Publication Data
A catalogue record for this book is available from the British Library.

ISBN 978-07509-4674-2

Picture credits: Historic photographs courtesy of Ian Boumphrey; modern photographs, author's collection. Maps courtesy of Birkenhead Central Library.

WITH THANKS TO
Christina Sutton
Glynis L.N Preston
Chris High
Tom Slemen
Birkenhead Central Library

Typeset in 10.5/13.5 Sabon
Printed and bound in England.

CONTENTS

Foreword 6

Introduction 7

A Deadly Dose	9	A Harmful Hesitation	65
An Unintended Libation	13	The Widow Worriers	67
Mersey Fireworks	15	The Bebington Showground Disaster	70
A Runaway Horse	18	A Dedicated Village	75
The Snow Woman	20	A Brave Mayor	77
The Exploding Boiler	21	A Devoted Brother	79
A Savage Scent	23	Rifle Respite	82
A New Ferry Fire	25	A Deep Sleep	84
A Crushing Commute	27	Sibling Adversity	86
Mournful Masonry	29	Starvation	89
Rabies	30	The Hoylake Special	91
The Tranmere Quarry Tragedy	32	An Epileptic End	93
A Fatal Omnibus	34	The Lost Boy	95
Sand Suffocation	36	A Shunting Tragedy	97
Clothes Combustion	39	A Plumber to the Rescue	99
The Tunnel Tot	41	A Cyclist's Claim	100
Observatory Plummet	43	The New Brighton Blaze	102
Munitions Maintenance	45	A Lamentable Labour	104
Out for the Count	47	Animal Cruelty	107
A Woeful Wash	50	A Lethal Toy	109
A Municipal Misfortune	52	Overexcited	111
A Guilty Porter	57	Mortal Elevation	114
The Calamity Cruise	59	A Day at the Races	116
A Hazardous Occupation	61	The Dangers of Naptha	118
An Imprudent Youth	62	Loaded	120
Guillotined	64	Undertaken	124

Index 126

FOREWORD

Charlie Chaplin, that great observer of the human situation, once remarked that life is a comedy in long-shot and a tragedy in close-up. This also applies to the individual throughout history. In long-shot the individual is just a statistic in a war, a plague, an earthquake, a pogrom, a fire or an accident. Six million Jews were exterminated by the Nazis, and each and every one of them was a person, exactly like you and me, but who were they? We know about a fraction of these people, but for most of us who flip thorugh history books, they shall remain anonymous victims of the Third Reich. The same is true of *Titanic* disaster, the atom bombings of Hiroshima and Nagasaki, and in more recent times the tsunami which killed 230,000 people on 26 December 2004 or the 2,749 people who died in the Twin Towers on that terrible day in September 2001; it's difficult to imagine death of that magnitude. Each of those people who perished in the towers or jumped to their death was someone's loved one.

Historians tend to ignore the life of the individual and deal instead with dates and the courses and causes of events. This macroscopic narrative often makes dull reading, and I have always been more intrigued with the lives of individuals and local and international history, rather than 1066 and the family trees of the Tudors and the succession of popes and Roman emperors.

In Wirral Tragic Tales, Daniel Longman has detailed the lives of everyday people who are not kings or queens, dukes or earls, all caught up in tragedy – something that affects us all in one form or another during our lives. In my opinion, this is true history, not some Act of Parliament or signing of a charter. Yes, parliamentary legislation affects people's lives, but a piece of paper or a world-changing idea is an inanimate and worthless thing unless people – like you and I – act upon that idea or enforce what was written on say, the Magna Carta. In this book there are fifty-two fascinating accounts of individuals falling victim to the circumstantial force of tragedy, and the stories range from the gruesome decapitation of a man by hydraulic machinery in 1899 to the tragic death of a woman whose garment burst into flames after accidentally coming into contact with the fire of the kitchen boiler. I have read every story in this book, and I applaud Daniel Longman for the sheer variety of the settings of these personal tragedies, but one story in particular, entitled 'Starvation' really touched my heart, and the tragic account made me wonder why there was never a revolution in Britain. I shall leave it to the reader to peruse that story in order to see where I'm coming from.

Tom Slemen

INTRODUCTION

What is a tragedy? There are a number of definitions, each with their own individual points to consider, but I'm sure that you will have your own understanding. There is the devastating loss of a family member, which as you read these words is affecting millions of people worldwide. This, the most common form of tragedy, is one that I'm sure you have experienced at least once in your lifetime. Such losses are private calamities, which become public knowledge only in the form of small black and white obituaries in local, and soon discarded, newspapers. Nevertheless, the disaster looms large for the relatives and friends of the dearly departed.

Then there are those collective disasters which tugs at the heartstrings of an entire town or city. The washout that was New Orleans in 2005 is a clear example of how this sort of tragedy can cause utter carnage for many. The effect of hurricane Katrina that year was most cataclysmic and long-lasting. The storm, which was one of the costliest hurricanes as well as one of the most deadly natural disasters in US history, brought heartache and sadness to many.

On a larger, and thankfully rarer scale, let's not forget the upheavals that cause chaos to whole countries, continents, and sometimes even the world. Wars raging across the whole of Europe, such as those unforgettable days of the early and mid-twentieth century caused misery for millions. The First World War alone created graves for an estimated eight million men, women and children. The worst tragedies are often man-made.

The human race has always had to cope with disaster. The people of Pompeii were literally burnt into the history books in 79 AD when the giant volcano Mount Vesuvius gushed forth layer upon layer of molten lava, bringing with it instant death. The Black Death of the fourteenth century brought pain and suffering in Britain from coast to coast. With a mortality rate of 30–75 per cent, the most common form of the disease, the bubonic plague, caused symptoms such as enlarged and inflamed lymph nodes, unbearable headaches, relentless nausea, incessantly aching joints, a high fever and repeated vomiting. Death was a happy release.

On 2 September 1666 the Great Fire of London swept across our nation's capital bringing destruction and devastation to many of its inhabitants. Eighty-seven churches were destroyed along with approximately 13,000 houses, the majority of which were built of inflammable timber and thatch. That disaster was brought about by the careless actions of a single baker.

Who could forget the Belfast-built vessel whose name today is etched into the consciousness of modern mankind? The *Titanic*, that colossal luxury liner which set off on its first and last ill-fated voyage in the month of April 1912. She became an overnight sensation, but for all the wrong reasons. That night over 1,000 passengers went down into the icy waters of the Atlantic and their deaths became the stuff of legends. The crew on board the *Titanic* are well-remembered for carrying out the Birkenhead Drill; 'Women and Children first!' This famous order was first carried out aboard HMS *Birkenhead* in the year 1852, when the 1,400-ton paddle-steamer became hopelessly impaled on an uncharted rock off the coast of South Africa. It was reported that of the 643 people on board the *Birkenhead*, only 193 were saved. Those who perished either drowned or were eaten by the great white sharks that are known to inhabit those savage waters. Because of the bravery and selfless sacrifice of the men on board all seven women and thirteen children were rowed away from the doomed wooden wreck to safety. I have not included this tale of gallantry in this book, since to condense an account of such heroism into a mere thousand words or so, would fail to do justice to those admirable men.

Indeed, it is often said that the worst situations bring out the best in people. While researching this book I have found an exceptionally high number of cases that support this claim. A prime example of such heroism took place in the year 1908, when four-year-old Henry Wilson bravely reached out to save his baby sister from drowning in Victoria Park, yet another was the valiant effort of Jabez Hughes who risked severe scalding in his attempt to rescue poor Ivy Williams at her house in Livingstone Street in 1913.

Of course these acts took place decades ago in a time that the majority of us never saw. However, they show us that a real sense of camaraderie and community spirit lies at the heart of society.

This was clearly demonstrated during the atrocities of 7 July 2005, when a series of coordinated bomb blasts struck London's public transport system during the morning rush hour. Fifty-two people were murdered in the attacks; the four terrorists known to have been involved also died, and about 700 innocent people were injured. This horrific crime brought people together in a united front, each helping those in need, whether they were stranger or friend. It is such acts of modern-day compassion that echo those of the times of *Titanic* and *Birkenhead*, and which will be remembered for generations to come.

Of course, such huge losses of life should be remembered, but lest we forget the local citizens that perished tragically, rescued valiantly, or witnessed some of the most amazing and remarkable sights that the Wirral has ever seen. It is these local tragedies which I have attempted to resurrect. The charming but often rose-tinted memories of Wirral's past have been recounted time and time again. We know about Laird's fantastic vision for the 'City of the Future'. We know of the marvellous work carried out by Lord Leverhulme and of his commendable industrial ambitions for Port Sunlight. We understand the niceties of Wirral and its illustrious history, but our peninsula's sometimes unpalatable past is often left unexplored.

The accidents and disasters featured in this book are all true, and they make saddening but nevertheless fascinating reading. Let us hope that such tragic occurrences are banished to the past. *C'est la vie.*

Daniel K. Longman

A DEADLY DOSE

On the evening of Saturday 1 April 1893, Frederick Clavey, an outdoor manager to a firm of ship painters, returned to his home at 51 Chestnut Grove, Tranmere. He had just completed a hard day's work and was keen to check up on his wife Dora, who had been very poorly since Easter Tuesday. On entering the house he made his way up the stairs to the master bedroom.

'Good evening dear', Frederick said cheerfully.

He noticed that his wife was fast asleep; understandably still feeling weak from the exhausting illness she was battling against. Strangely, she was lying face down.

Frederick quietly walked over to Dora and took hold of her hand. 'Are you going to get up dear?'

Frederick's heart skipped a beat as he realised that something was very wrong with his wife. She was not moving and did not even appear to be breathing. Mr Clavey at once rushed out of the bedroom and down the stairs, much to the astonishment of

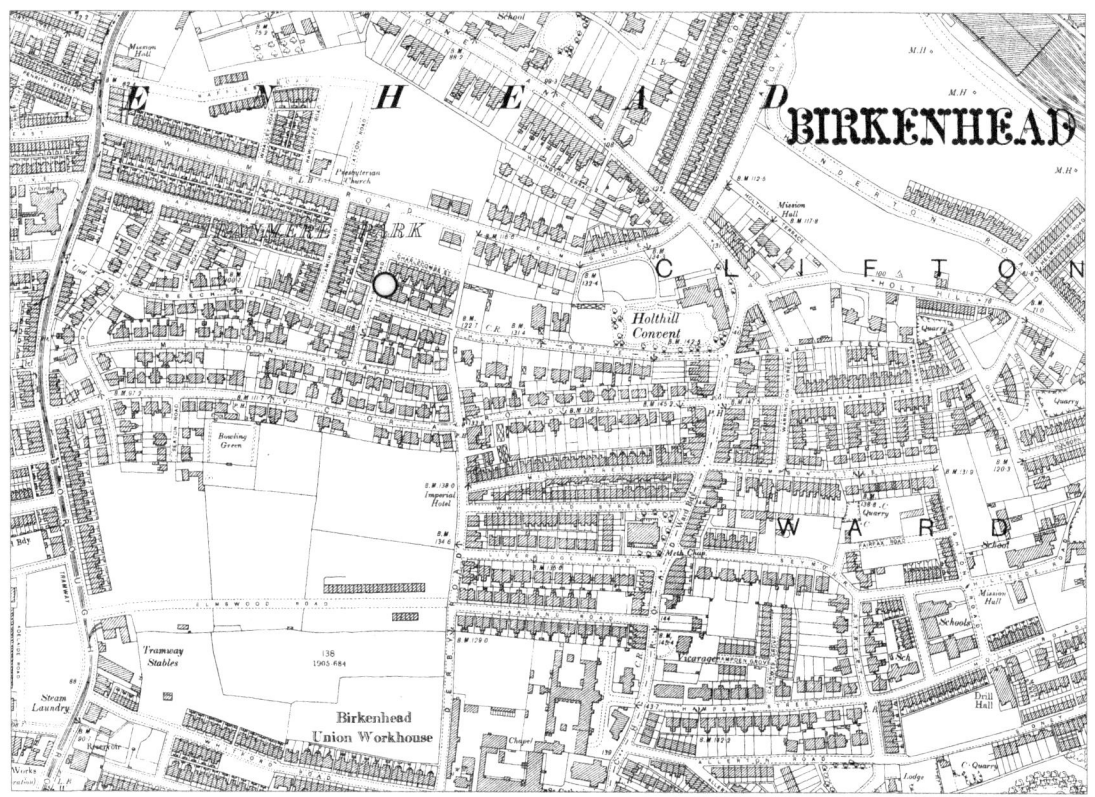

Chestnut Grove, Tranmere, taken from a map dated 1899.

his three young children, the two servant girls and Dora's younger brother. Without a word, Frederick flew out of the front door at a tremendous pace and into the street in search of Dora's physician, Dr William Johnston. The speed of Frederick's actions caused him to slip on the kerb, painfully spraining his ankle as he fell awkwardly onto the road. He gritted his teeth and hobbled across Derby Road to find the doctor on the doorstep of his home at 2 Elm Grove.

Frederick quickly described his wife's seemingly comatose state to the doctor and the two of them immediately rushed back to Chestnut Grove.

The doctor went into the bedroom and conducted a swift examination of Mrs Clavey. His face soon registered a look of terrible confusion and perplexity. The doctor's expression confirmed Frederick's worst fear; his wife was dead.

Doctor Johnston was left utterly bewildered at how Dora had died so suddenly. Only earlier that morning he had spoken to her and she seemed quite merry and alert. He searched the bed and discovered a small half-empty bottle under the pillow. It was labelled, 'Poison, chloroform. R.D Evans, chemist'. His professional nose detected the unmistakable scent of chloroform, but he had never prescribed it. Dr Johnston searched further, suspecting that perhaps Mrs Clavey had used a handkerchief to administer the medicine herself. However he could find nothing of the sort and thus suspected the woman, who was now lying dead only a matter of inches away from him, to have drunk the poison straight from the bottle.

On Monday 3 April an inquest into the death of the twenty-two year old was formally opened at the Park Hotel, Charing Cross. After hearing what had happened that sad Saturday night, the coroner, Dr Churton, enquired about the actual cause of Mrs Clavey's death.

'Had your wife been in the habit of taking medication independent of what might have been prescribed?' he asked Mr Clavey.

'Some two years ago, when she had a serious illness, I heard something of that, but up to the present date I heard nothing whatever of it; in fact, I was fully under the impression there was nothing of the sort, but the doctor since tells me there has been something of that kind.'

Dr Johnston himself was then questioned.

'Had you any reason to suspect she had taken an overdose?'

'That was the only way I could explain what I saw after I found the bottle and from the position she was lying in.' he replied.

The coroner continued, 'Now, assuming that the bottle was full, would half of it be sufficient to destroy life?'

The doctor nodded. 'Yes sir; if it was not given properly and carefully watched it would kill them.'

Bella McGuinness, an eighteen-year-old girl who had been employed as nurse to the Claveys for sixteen months was next to be questioned.

She deposed that between two and half-past on that Saturday afternoon, her mistress gave her a note and a small bottle in an envelope. She said that she was told to take them to Mr Evans the chemist in Greenway Road. Bella claimed that she had

51 Chestnut Grove as it looks today.

not seen the bottle before, but it was not the first time she had been sent on such an errand. On her return Bella recalled that she handed the bottle to Mrs Clavey and left her to rest. She stated that she had visited the bedroom three or four times after. The first such occasion she claimed to have heard Mrs Clavey breathing very heavily, almost as if she was sobbing in her sleep.

'Have you ever heard her breathe so heavily before?' the coroner asked.

'No sir, I did not. That was about half-past three.'

Robert Daniel Evans, a forty-year-old chemist and druggist, was called to be questioned. He stated that he could remember Bella McGuinness coming into his store at 5 Greenway Road and handing him an envelope with a bottle and a note. It read,

'A shilling's worth of chloroform, Mrs Clavey'

'Have you ever prescribed the stuff before?' Mr Evans was asked.

'Several times.'

'The same quantity?'

'Yes, a shilling's worth, an ounce.'

The coroner was keen to understand all of the facts.

'How long was it since you supplied it before?'

'They came four times last week. I refused it twice, and gave it twice.'

The coroner persisted and maintained his torrent of questions.

'Had Mrs Clavey ever fetched it herself?'

'Yes sir. If I refused anybody else, she would come next day and get some other things, amongst them camphorated oil. She used to say she was going to mix the oil with the chloroform for rubbing.'

With all the answers given, the coroner began summing up the case. He was of the firm belief that the deceased had evidently taken a deadly dose of poison, and no doubt had taken it to relieve the pain she had been suffering from for a considerable period of time. The jury might say that she took poison, and that when she took it Mrs Clavey knew that she was committing suicide. On the other hand, they may believe that the woman had inadvertently taken an overdose for the sole purpose of relieving pain. For his own part Dr Churton did not feel inclined to believe Dora had taken the poison to take her own life.

'No, no. She did not do it intentionally!' a juror interrupted.

The jury soon returned a verdict that Mrs Clavey died from an overdose of poison, inadvertently taken.

AN UNINTENDED LIBATION

On the afternoon of 28 May 1913 Mr Kay of 4 Water Street was driving a horse and cart down Market Street, Birkenhead. He was employed by the brewery Mackie and Gladstone, and was transporting a number of casks filled with beer and minerals from the factory in Hamilton Street.

At the junction of Argyle Street, Mr Kay took a firm grip of the reins and ordered his two horses to trot across the thoroughfare. As the cart was crossing the second set of lines built into the road, a large tram, the number 51 bogey car, came hastily towards it. On seeing the cart the conductor quickly applied the brakes, causing the many passengers on board to jolt forward in their seats. For a moment or two it appeared as if the tram would clear, but as the screech of the breaks cried out, the cart was flung mightily towards the pavement in one swift hit. The horses were shaken and appeared quite disturbed, but Mr Kay was unharmed and was quick to

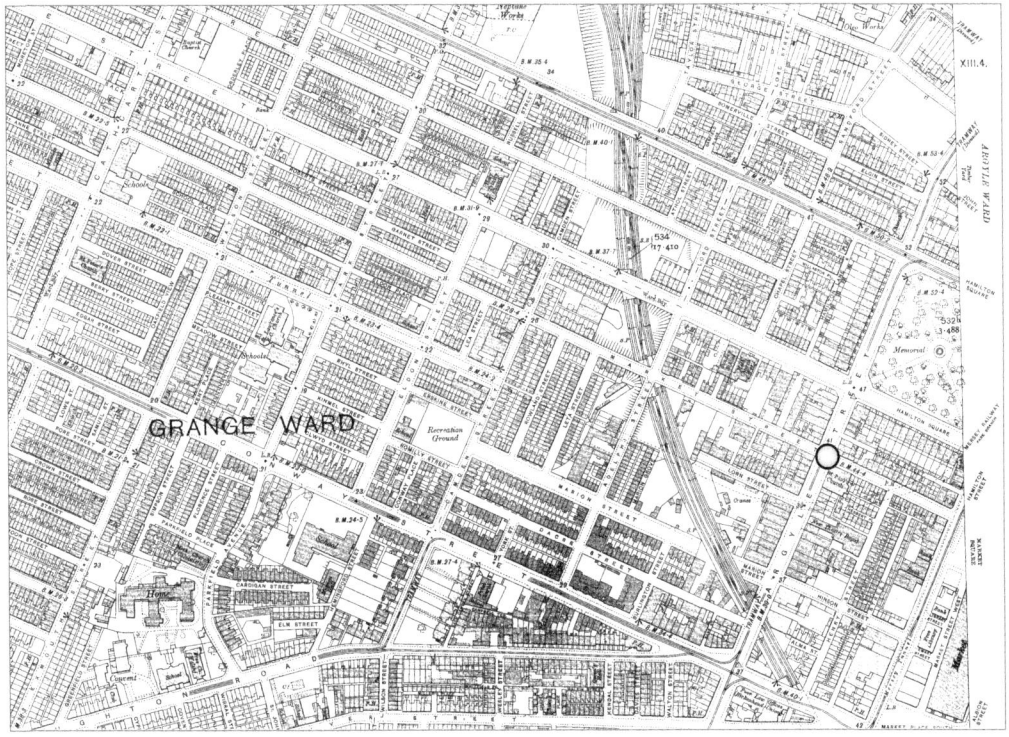

The junction of Market Street and Argyle Street, Birkenhead, 1912.

The view down Argyle Street with the junction in question in the distance, c. 1900.

The corner of Market Street and Argyle Street, 2007.

keep them under control. The cart's rear wheel was jammed against the pavement before ultimately breaking off, causing the casks to tumble and fall onto the road. The force of the fall caused beer to flow copiously down Argyle Street, as broken bottles lay strewn across the whole street. The flowing liquor gave the accident a more serious appearance than was warranted, and soon a large crowd had gathered around the alcohol-laden puddles to take a closer look at the afternoon mishap.

Traffic was brought to a standstill as the cart was eventually carried away, minus a wheel, by a number of local men. The tram was not damaged and continued on its way to Woodside.

MERSEY FIREWORKS

In the year 1864 one of the most destructive scenes the Wirral has ever seen took place. Scores of people living on both sides of the river witnessed the terrible yet breathtaking incident that caused widespread fear and panic throughout the area.

On the cold winter's night of 15 January the *Lottie Sleigh*, an African trading barque was moored on the Mersey. She was being loaded with supplies from the Tranmere magazine boats; these included a total of eleven tons of gunpowder.

At about six o'clock, a ship's steward entered the captain's cabin and began trimming the paraffin oil lamps. As he was preparing to light the lamp nearest to the captain's bed, the oil spilt and ignited, and soon flames took hold of the captain's bed

Woodside Ferry, Birkenhead, on a map dated 1870.

A depiction of the explosion as reported in the Illustrated London News.

curtains. The steward promptly attempted to extinguish the blaze, but the fire had already begun to spread at an alarming rate. He cried out, warning his fellow crew members of the dire situation. No doubt the knowledge that so much flammable powder was in the hold somewhat paralysed the actions of all the men aboard the doomed vessel. They gathered together what they could and clambered onto smaller craft whose captains had come to their aid.

The roar of the fire was deafening and throughout the whole dreadful affair the pitiful yelps of a small dog could be heard coming from the wooden inferno.

As the crew reached dry land, news had already spread around the pier heads that the *Lottie Sleigh* was sure to blow. By seven o'clock hundreds of people had gathered at Woodside, eager to see the amazing spectacle that was unfolding in the distance.

At 7.20 pm, the fire finally reached the great mass of explosives. The powder began to spark, and high-pitched shrieks could be heard by the excited crowds on shore.

Suddenly, the night sky was lit up by a brilliant white light as the stricken ship exploded in a ferocious blast of debris. The blistering orange flames appeared to lick the stars as fire shot up to an extraordinary height. Neighbouring vessels rocked violently and struggled to stay afloat as forceful waves crashed mercilessly against their bows.

Woodside Landing Stage, 2007.

Nearby buildings also felt the force; many had their windows blown out, causing shards of glass to shower down onto the streets and the watchful public below. The night lamps were all at once extinguished, plunging the dockside into an eerie darkness. Nuts and bolts whistled through the air, many being flung all the way into Tranmere. More debris fell from the sky onto the quayside, causing many to run for cover from the downpour of flaming timber.

The hordes of onlookers gasped as the immensity of the blast overwhelmed them. A number ran panic-stricken from the landing stage towards the apparent safety of the town. The town, however, was not safe. The gigantic vertical block of the ship's bow, the knee, rocketed through the sky and straight into the moulding room of Mr Clayton, a ship builder. At a house in Sydney Street, a heavy iron component crashed through the roof, narrowly missing three young children inside. In North Street a similar incident occurred when a long metal bar fell through a roof, causing minor damage.

The majority of properties in Hamilton Street, Argyle Street, Chester Street and Church Street had their windows blown out by the blast, causing an immense amount of damage and costs to their owners. Scores of residents rushed from their homes to find out what had happened. Some people feared that a gas explosion had occurred. However they were soon to discover that gas was not the cause of the almost apocalyptic events that they had just experienced. Nevertheless many gas lines had been fractured, causing small fires to erupt across the Wirral and Liverpool coasts.

Amazingly, no lives were lost during destruction of the *Lottie Sleigh* and her smouldering wreckage was eventually brought ashore.

A RUNAWAY HORSE

At about half-past ten on the evening of Friday 12 May 1900, Mr Finnegan was driving a horse and wagon full of men from Eastham to Rock Ferry. His job was to ferry workmen to and from their homes for work in the villages early in the morning and late at night.

On that cold and frosty night, he held the reigns tightly and carefully guided his horse as it trotted briskly along the dimly lit streets of Bromborough. As they were passing Bromborough Pool, the horse became agitated and Finnegan tugged at the leather straps of the bridle in an attempt to calm the animal. However, truly terrified at something, the horse proceeded to gallop at a tremendous pace down the road towards New Ferry. As the horse picked up speed and raced erratically through the town, Finnegan was unseated and thrown to the ground. Clutching his side, he watched as his wagon disappeared into the night.

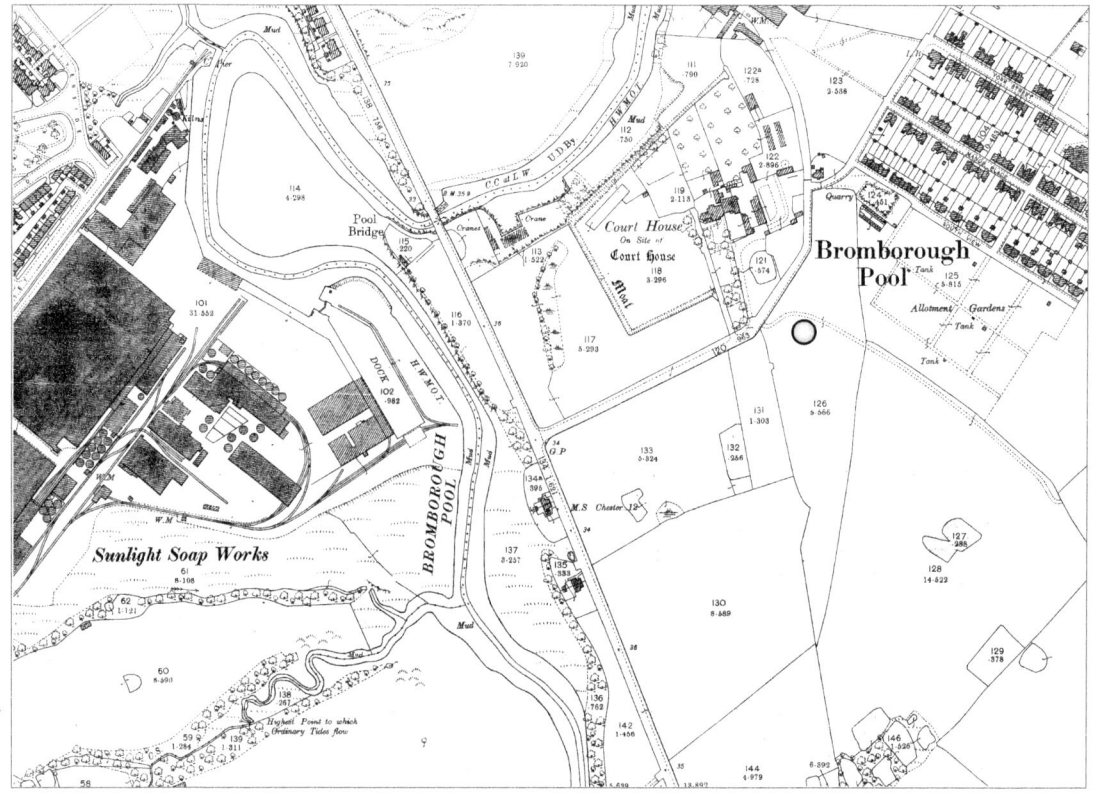

The vicinity of Bromborough Pool, as seen on a map from 1899.

Seconds later Mr Taylor, one of the workers travelling in the vehicle, was thrown out, closely followed by workmate Mr Allen, who upon falling appeared to have broken his leg. An ambulance from Birkenhead was called and soon arrived at the scene. The ambulance men took Finnegan and Allen to the Borough Hospital where it was found that Mr Finnegan had painfully bruised and cut his face, while Mr Allen had suffered contused wounds to his knee. Fortunately Mr Taylor was unhurt by the fall and given a clean bill of health.

Meanwhile the runaway horse continued to gallop driverless through the small town of New Ferry. As it entered the busy neighbourhood, people fled into their houses to avoid being crushed by the uncontrollable creature, which had now covered almost a distance of 2 miles.

William Dodwell, a twenty-nine-year-old sanitary official was walking along the road when he heard shouting and the familiar sound of horses' hooves, only this time much louder and faster than usual. Turning around, William caught sight of the horse about to crash into him, and with lightning reflexes the young hospital worker quickly stepped back and narrowly avoided being killed by the beast. Quickly gathering his composure he chased after the carriage and managed to get a foot onto the back step. To the shocked eyes of onlookers he bravely climbed into the driver's seat where he grasped hold of the reins and pulled hard, successfully bringing the frightened horse to a halt a further 2 miles up the road in Chester Street. A round of applause went up, and William Dodwell was cheered not only by the residents in the street but also by the workers still trapped in the carriage, who had just endured their most terrifying ride home!

THE SNOW WOMAN

On the night of Saturday 5 January 1867, Mr William Rainford, an elderly farmer living at the Grange, near to West Kirby, retired to bed at about half-past nine. He left his aged wife in the kitchen, expecting her to come and join him in bed in a short while. As usual, William dozed off to sleep.

Later, at about half-past eleven, William awoke to find that his wife had still not come to bed. Worried, he got up and went down to the kitchen. There he found a candle burning on the windowsill, but his wife was nowhere to be seen. He searched for her throughout the entire house, but still his elderly spouse could not be found. Now very concerned, Mr Rainford awoke his servants and together they searched the farm outhouses in the hope that she may have wandered into one of those. Despite their thorough investigations Mrs Rainford still could not be found. The police constable of the district was contacted but even he could shed no further light upon the matter. The poor old man was in a very sad state and spent a miserable and sleepless night racked with worry.

It wasn't until daybreak that the shocking truth about the disappearance of Mrs Rainford was revealed. At half-past eight on the Sunday morning, the frozen body of the eighty-nine-year-old was found lying near to the house, completely covered in snow; her wrinkled skin had turned a pale blue.

It was supposed that during the night Mrs Rainford had ventured outside to use the water closet, which was near to where she was found, when a strong gust of wind blew the infirm woman down onto the frosty ground below. With no strength to rise, she was soon covered in the winter snow as it fell down heavily from above.

The prevailing snowstorm that weekend was a particularly fierce one and was no doubt responsible for Mrs Rainford's icy death.

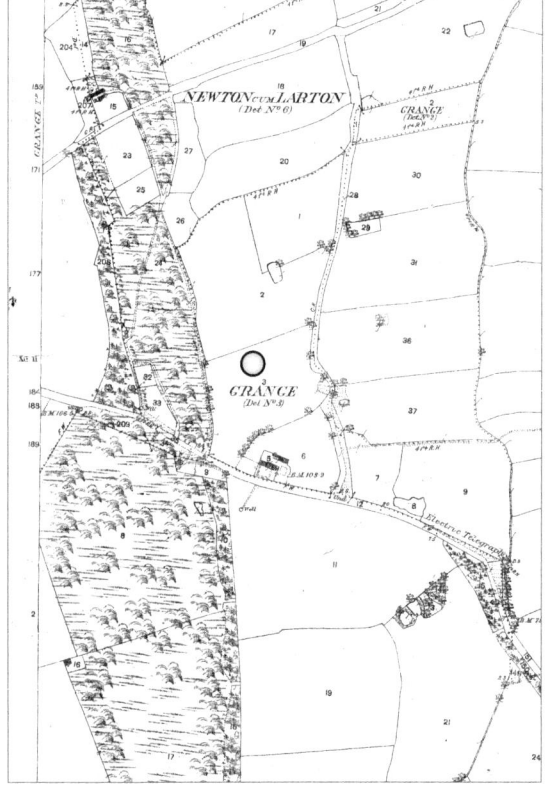

The Grange, West Kirby, on a map dated 1870.

THE EXPLODING BOILER

The long frost of January 1893 was particularly unpleasant and was to be the cause of a tragic death of a Rock Ferry housewife. Twenty-three-year-old Sarah Bishop was the wife of school headmaster Mr J. Bishop, who taught on the *Akbar*, a reformatory school ship moored in the Mersey.

On the afternoon of Thursday 5 January Mrs Bishop was busy with the housework at her home at 52 Mersey Road. At about three o'clock she began hanging some clothes up to dry on a line in the kitchen, which stretched in front of the fireplace across to the other side of the living room at a height of about 10ft.

All of a sudden the house began to shudder, quickly followed by a terrific explosion. The blast caused the fireplace to blow out from the wall with great power, causing immense damage throughout the whole room. The might of the force had rendered Mrs Bishop unconscious and light poured over her limp body through the gaping hole which now gave onto the alleyway alongside the house.

Fourteen-year-old Joseph Poole, Mr Bishop's attendant, was in the parlour, and upon hearing the explosion ran into the kitchen to see what had happened. The room was full of steam and smoke and after only a brief search Joseph was forced to retreat to catch his breath. On composing himself the youngster returned to the scene of destruction. Upon entering for a second time, Joseph could hear the faint groans of Mrs Bishop as she lay injured beneath the rubble. He gallantly began to remove the bricks, plaster and even the oven which covered Sarah, and heaved her out of the debris. With great care, the youth carried the unconscious woman out into the safety of the parlour and placed her gently down on the sofa. He then ran out into the street to seek help.

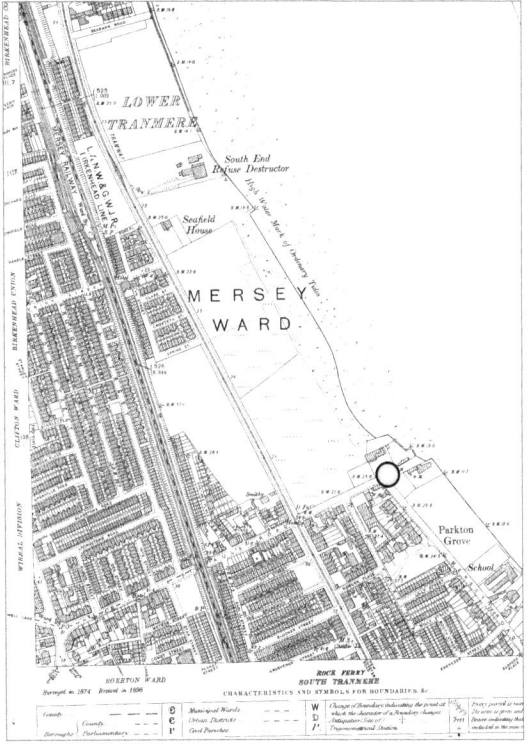

Mersey Road, Rock Ferry, on a map dated 1899.

Mersey Road in Rock Ferry, c. 1910, where the Bishops resided.

Outside, he found Mr Booth walking by, and at once called for him to help his master's wife. Luckily the passing man had had experience working as an ambulance attendant and was able to assist the wounded woman until a doctor could be sought.

Not long afterwards Dr Pearson and Dr Robson arrived to treat the injured Mrs Bishop, whom they found to be suffering from shock and a number of internal injuries. Through their assistance Mrs Bishop managed to recover consciousness but sadly died between nine and ten o'clock that evening.

On investigation it was discovered that the boiler, which lay battered in the corner of the kitchen, contained several inches of ice and both pipes were frozen. The pressure caused by the icy blockage was undoubtedly the cause of the explosion that afternoon.

An inquest held at the Royal Standard Hotel before the coroner Mr Churton returned a verdict of accidental death, and a total of 4*s* 9*d* was collected for Joseph Poole in recognition of his brave and heroic efforts.

A SAVAGE SCENT

A rather unusual inquest was held at the Abbotsford Hotel, Seacombe, on 19 August 1896. That afternoon a case of severe canine viciousness was brought to light as the death of forty-nine-year-old Christopher Ellsworth was investigated. Amelia Ellsworth, daughter of the deceased, was the first and only witness to give evidence.

She stated that on the recent bank holiday her father went to see his St Bernard dog which was kept in the back yard of his house at 23 Rudgrave Square. It was at times known to be a very savage animal and Miss Ellsworth remarked that it was really only she who could control it. The dog was nearly two years old and had only been outside a few times. It did not get much exercise; the first time they attempted to take it out for a walk it had knocked over a child in the street.

On the afternoon in question it was heard that she had joined her father in the yard and that she had taken a whip with her in case the animal became raucous.

Rudgrave Square on a map from 1899.

Rudgrave Square, where Mr Ellsworth was viciously attacked.

Amelia recalled how almost as soon as Christopher stepped foot in the yard the dog charged and seized him by the leg. The creature snarled and shook its mammoth head from side to side, dragging its frightened owner down to the concrete. Amelia stated that she had begun hitting the dog with the whip but to no avail. Several frightening minutes passed in which the woman managed to move the dog away a total of three times by holding it by its salvia-ridden jaws. But the attacker was too powerful and it proceeded to persist in snarling, biting and pinning its master to the ground. Ultimately, Miss Ellsworth described how she was forced to summon all her might and heave the animal's skull in-between the nearby door frame. Several pitiful yelps were heard to moan out of the psychotic pet as Amelia slammed its head as hard as she could between the frame and backdoor. This and the beating with the whip, successfully forced the dog to surrender her father, who was by that time badly injured with his left leg dripping with blood.

They both hurried into the safety of the house and a doctor was called to the property at once.

The jury heard that on the previous Thursday, Mr Ellsworth, after being in the care of Dr Cook and a nurse, was removed to Seacombe Cottage Hospital.

Sarah Collins, matron of the hospital, stated that Mr Ellsworth's cause of death was exhaustion from continued sickness due to dog bites. She remarked that her former patient's left leg was very badly injured, having been torn by the dog's teeth.

In answer to the coroner, Miss Ellsworth stated that on the day of the attack her father had not done anything to provoke or annoy the animal, yet there was one thing that may have caused the dog to become animated. Amelia said that earlier that day her father had been to the lairages, and there was a strong possibility that the scent of blood on his boots roused the animal's temper and resulted in the violent attack.

The jury returned a verdict that death was due to the effects of dog bites. The St Bernard was shot.

A NEW FERRY FIRE

On the evening of 13 August 1840, Miss Mary Ann Cowper, who was originally from Nottingham, arrived at her lodgings in New Ferry after returning from a short visit to Liverpool. She was a pretty young woman and was said to be very kind and pleasant to all who knew her. Miss Cowper dressed in the most beautiful styles of the day and often caught the eye of many local bachelors. However, these men could only watch from afar, as Miss Cowper was spoken for. In the coming January she was to be married; a union that would bring her £600 a year. Recently, however, the families of Miss Cowper and her fiancé had had a disagreement and the two had been forced temporarily to separate. In the meantime the young lady had been lodging at various respectable houses in the locality until she could be reunited with her husband-to-be.

It was about eight o'clock when Miss Cowper returned to the house, and as usual she settled in for the night and had some supper. As she did so the elderly landlady Mrs Sankey, spoke with her and they exchanged pleasant conversation about their day as they were accustomed to do. Once she had finished her evening meal, Miss Cowper lit a small candle and made her way up the stairs to her room overlooking the Mersey. Hers was the best bedroom in the house and Miss Cowper also occupied an adjoining sitting room, both of which she had lived in for about two months.

Soon afterwards Mrs Sankey and her servant extinguished all of the candles in the downstairs rooms and bade each other goodnight.

All was well until the early hours when Mrs Sankey was awoken from her slumber by a loud crackling sound. The elderly landlady listened more closely and heard the sound again, this time becoming much more alarmed. The clock struck two as Mrs Sankey arose from her bed and hurried out onto the landing. She urgently followed the sounds and soon found flames issuing from beneath the door of Miss Cowper's room. In a

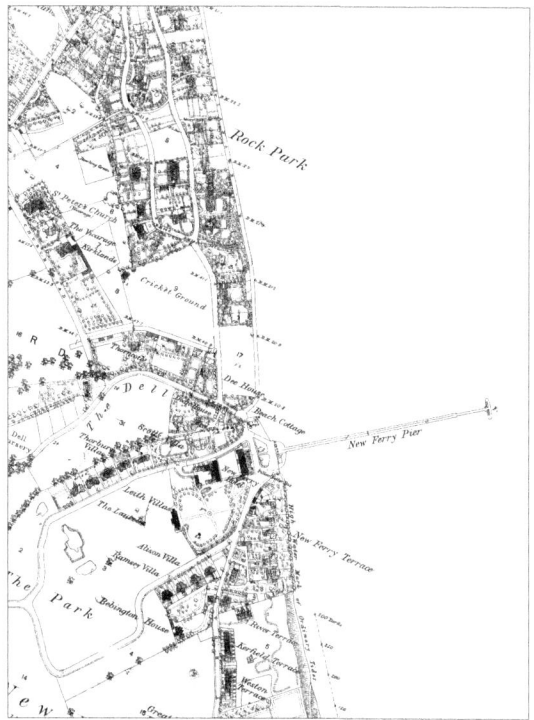

The vicinity of New Ferry, dated 1870.

state of terrible fear she roused her teenage servant girl before they both fled the property.

Mr Hayes, who resided at the Liverpool Custom House opposite to Mrs Sankey's property, heard the commotion and rushed out to offer his assistance. Upon hearing the news a neighbouring woman ran up the road, knocking door to door to see if anyone could help rescue Mary Ann Cowper, who was presumably still trapped inside. Mr Ostle, a joiner, and three of his young apprentices were soon on the scene. They found the house to be in a state of rapid combustion, with flames pouring out from the upstairs bedroom. The four men entered the building and Mr Hayes was the first to burst open the door as he and his apprentices made a desperate attempt to save the stricken young lady inside. But the intensity of the fire drove them back and it soon became apparent that there was no hope for Miss Cowper. In a matter of moments the room began to crumble under the intense heat and the floorboards gave way. The blackened body of Miss Cowper crashed down into the room below, along with the smouldering bed and surrounding furniture. She was dead.

Later that morning Miss Cowper was found face down among the rubble. Her body had become a black carbonised mass, with part of her skull entirely destroyed.

It was supposed that the unfortunate woman had fallen asleep with a candle still burning and that it had somehow set alight the bedclothes or curtains. Her remains were removed to the parlour until they could be interred.

A CRUSHING COMMUTE

On the night of 19 July 1913, Percy Banks, a forty-four-year-old french polisher, left his home at 3 Lee Road, Hoylake. He was on his way to the station to see his sister and brother-in-law depart by the 10.15pm train later that evening. He was known to be a temperate man who very rarely drank. His appearance to some was comical; his right leg being slightly shorter than the other due to a diseased hip which caused him no end of trouble. Nevertheless, Percy made his way down to the platform in a steady and stable manner. The station was bustling with people that night and among them sat Madge Silcock and her friend Bessie Derbyshire. The two ladies had come down to see friends depart by the same train. Miss Derbyshire was standing near to the carriage doorway trying to pass on some last minute goodbyes as Miss Silcock sat on a seat at the far end of the platform. She noticed Percy Banks standing at the door of the next carriage, in a similar position to Bessie.

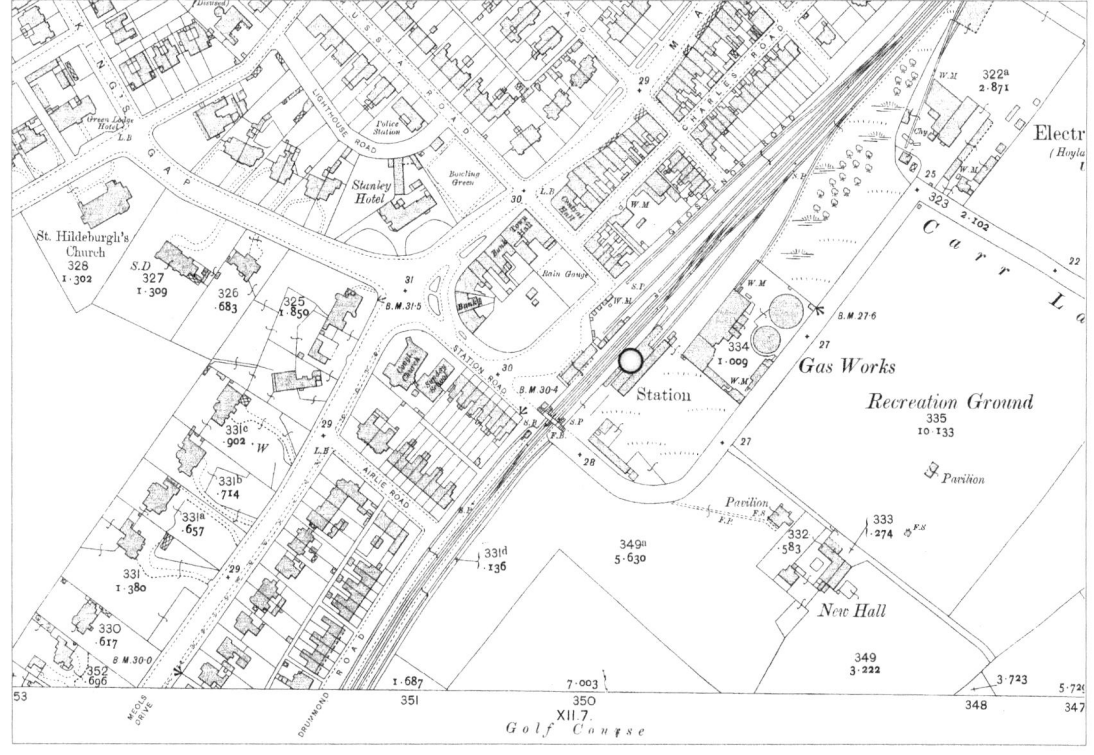

Hoylake station on a map from 1912.

The location where Percy Banks lost his life, c. 1910.

Just then the train began to judder and it prepared to move away down the track. The mass of people stepped back to the safety of the platform as the large iron wheels began to rotate.

However Mr Banks failed to retreat. To Miss Derbyshire it appeared that his coat was stuck and Percy struggled desperately to remove himself from the swiftly moving locomotive. Suddenly, he disappeared from view between the carriages.

No one could catch hold of him, it all happened so fast. Arthur Worth, a railway guard on his way home, witnessed the incident from his position at the train window. He would later state that Mr Banks had fallen as if he had been 'shot out of a gun.'

At the platform, a number of people soon began to realise what had happened.

'Oh Bessie, look at that man; he is on the line!' Miss Silcock gasped as she put her hand to her mouth in horror. The two ladies got up and joined the crowd who had hurried towards Mr Banks. They saw that he was trapped in between two carriages, lying across the buffers. Bessie ran to fetch help and caught the attention of William Tottey, a ticket collector. He was just about to alter the indicators for the next train when the panicking woman came running up towards him. She informed Mr Tottey of what she had seen and the pair ran over and shuffled their way through the anxious crowd. Mr Tottey found the man in an awful state. Percy was lying across the metal rails, his right leg between them and his left stretched towards the platform. His head was between the points. A doctor was called but it was found that the train had passed across Mr Banks' body, straight over his diseased hip. Death would have been almost instantaneous.

The following Tuesday an inquest into the unfortunate end of Percy Banks was held at Hoylake police station where a jury returned a verdict of accidental death.

MOURNFUL MASONRY

The awful fatality of one Tranmere youngster took place on 4 February 1913. The little boy, Samuel Shaw, was out playing with his friends near to his home at 25 Mill Street. At about four o'clock, Samuel was standing at the corner of Derby Road and Whitfield Street, watching a large horse-drawn cart trotting along just a few feet in front of him and his playmates. The cart contained heavy mortar and the vigilant driver was guiding the vehicle with the utmost caution. All of a sudden the horse backed without warning, forcing the rear of the cart to crash into a garden wall. It collapsed with an almighty clamour, as did the gate attached to it. Poor Samuel was thrown to the ground and in the blink of an eye was obscured from view beneath a mountain of masonry. So dangerous was the incident that another boy's jersey was torn; the sleeve being ripped wide open. He had had a lucky escape!

Horrified bystanders rushed to the roadside where they immediately began to remove the broken bricks and retrieved the child's grazed and bruised body. Without further delay he was picked up and carried to the house of Dr Wyse. Regrettably, death was swift and Samuel Shaw's brief and innocent existence had been cut short. The doctor pronounced life extinct and the body was sent to the mortuary.

A map showing the corner of Mill Street and Derby Road, dated 1912.

The father of the deceased was an employee at shipbuilders Cammell Laird and Co. It had been just a month since he had lost his wife and only a fortnight since the passing of another one of his children. It was to be a sad homecoming that night when he discovered that yet another member of his family had been cruelly taken from him.

RABIES

The month of April 1877 saw widespread fear stretch across the Wirral as dreadful rumours of diseased dogs became rife. At a sitting of the County Magistrates on Thursday 12 April the case of thirty-five year old Elizabeth Rimmer of Helmingham Road, Tranmere, was brought to light. It was heard that in the middle of February the woman had been bitten on the finger by a little dog her husband had brought into the house. The wound bled slightly at the time, but afterwards healed. However over the coming weeks Mrs Rimmer began to complain of awful pains spreading to different parts of her body. At the time no one suspected that the tiny wound she received from the canine was the cause of such aches, but on 11 April Mrs Rimmer's symptoms worsened. She developed violent spasms, hyperactivity and confusion, as well as high fever, an irregular heartbeat and strained breathing. Dr Ricketts was called to conduct an examination and at once diagnosed

Helmingham Road as seen on a map from 1870.

her with hydrophobia, also known as Rabies, a serious viral infection of the central nervous system, transmitted by the bite of an infected animal. As her condition continued to deteriorate, Dr Ricketts was assisted by Drs Lambert and Ryan, but their efforts were to no avail. It was heard that on the morning of Thursday 12 April, at about nine o'clock, Elizabeth Rimmer succumbed to the disease and died.

The magistrates that afternoon issued a pressing order that all domestic dogs were to be kept carefully fastened up and any stray mutts found were to be quarantined for two months. There had recently been reports of dogs at large that were believed to be mad; one that had bitten several others was known to be rabid. Unfortunately, not all of theses dogs were successfully caught and a small number of people had since become infected.

The following week an inquest into the death of Elizabeth Rimmer was held at the Queens Arms Hotel, Holt Hill. The only additional piece of evidence produced was that the dog which bit the deceased had itself been bitten by its own mother which later proved to be rabid and had been destroyed. The coroner remarked that, under the circumstances, the action of the magistrates in forbidding all dogs to be at large was highly commendable. The jury returned a verdict that Mrs Rimmer died of hydrophobia caused by the bite of a dog.

THE TRANMERE QUARRY TRAGEDY

On the afternoon of Wednesday 23 July 1913, thirty-seven-year-old Ellen Pleavin was at her home at 49 Holt Road, Tranmere. Just before noon she realised that she had not seen her young son, Frankie, for some time. Ellen went outside to see if he was there, but could not find him. A neighbour called over to Mrs Pleavin and informed her that she had seen her boy playing near to the disused quarry in Sidney Road. Ellen thanked the neighbour and walked the short distance to the Davies Quarry, as it was known, which was nearby. On arriving at the site Mrs Pleavin could see no sign of her son, so thinking that he may have been playing down in the quarry yard, she looked over in the hope of spotting him there.

On looking down Mrs Pleavin became dizzy. The sheer depth of the quarry caused her to become light-headed and all at once she lost her balance. The disorientated woman let out a scream as she fell 120ft or so down into a blackened mountain of ash.

Hilda Haines of 53 Holt Road was in her bathroom at the time of the incident. Her house overlooked the quarry and she had noticed Mrs Pleavin peering over the quarry edge before hearing her desperate cry. Upon realising that the woman was now nowhere to be seen, she assumed that she must have toppled over. Mrs Haines hurried out into Mersey Park and contacted PC Stephenson who was on duty that afternoon.

Together they ran to the site and upon seeing the trapped woman immediately ran for an ambulance. On returning the constable found George Nightingale and another

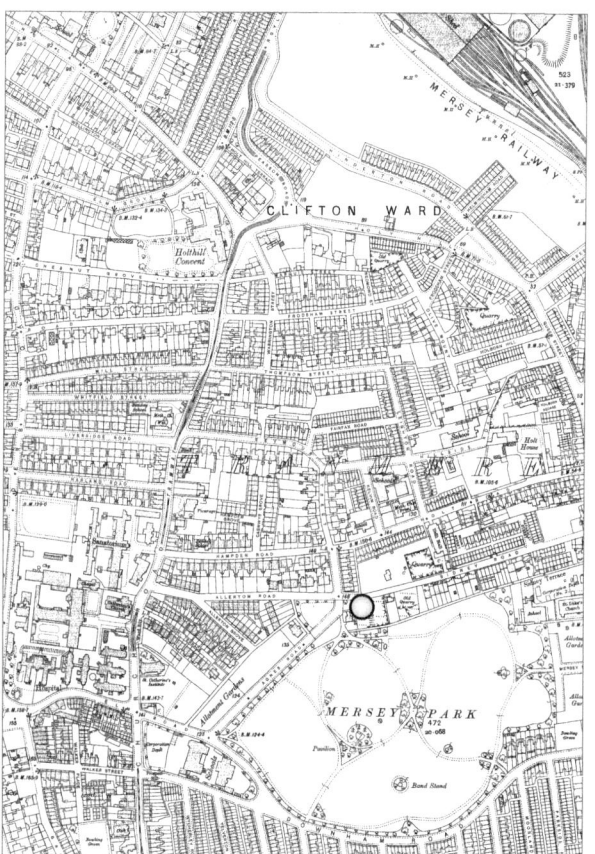

A 1912 map showing Sidney Road, Tranmere.

local man who had also heard Mrs Pleavin's scream, climbing down into the quarry with a ladder. On the ridge a large crowd had begun to assemble, all of whom were eager to discover what had taken place. As the anxious mass waited, the question of how to raise Mrs Pleavin to the surface presented itself. At first it appeared that the only way to get the woman out of the quarry was through the use of a series of ladders, but that would be a dangerous and risky option. When the ambulance men arrived it was decided that the most practical method of rescuing Mrs Pleavin would be through the use of a derrick, a type of crane that could be used to hoist Mrs Pleavin from the rubble and out to safety.

As the male onlookers began erecting the rescue crane, the ambulance staff hurried to the base of the quarry and examined Mrs Pleavin as best they could. They found her to be suffering from a fractured thigh bone and also to be badly bruised about the arms.

After working for an hour or so everything was in order to begin the precarious action of raising Mrs Pleavin from the mound of ash. The word was given, and with great care the distressed woman was brought to the top of the quarry without causing further injury.

News of the accident spread quickly and by the time Ellen was brought to the surface, an even larger crowd, including Mr James Pleavin, had gathered at the brink of the quarry. On reaching the top, Ellen shocked onlookers by being perfectly conscious despite her terrific fall. 'I was looking for Frankie', she cried, as her husband rushed to the front of the mass.

Ellen was immediately taken to the Borough Hospital where she was examined by the junior house surgeon Dr Mackenzie. He found her to be suffering from a fracture of the neck, fracture of the femur and several broken ribs. For the rest of the afternoon Mrs Pleavin's health seemed stable and she reiterated to medical staff that she had gone to the quarry to see if she could find her son, but had turned giddy while looking over the edge. Her husband was thankful that she was still alive; it was miraculous that anyone could have sustained such a fall and lived to tell the tale.

However James's joy was short-lived. Later that evening his wife's health took a turn for the worse and at about half-past six Ellen died from shock. On the following Friday, an inquest into the death of Ellen Pleavin was formally opened by the Borough Coroner Mr Cecil Holden. It was there that a jury returned a verdict of accidental death, and PC Stephenson and George Nightingale were both praised for their valiant action. It was heard that little Frankie Pleavin was subsequently found playing in Mersey Park, blissfully unaware of the worry and distress that his disappearance had caused.

A FATAL OMNIBUS

On the morning of 4 August 1887, Thomas Stokes was riding from his home in Mount Road, New Brighton, to Seacombe on the 8.30am omnibus owned by Mr Gardiner. The young man was sitting on the front seat nearest to the driver, who carefully guided the imposing machine through the early morning streets of Wallasey.

As they drove up Brougham Road, Mr Stokes spotted an elderly lady walking along the footpath. She was widower Mrs Isabella Hepburn, and he estimated her to be about 8–10yds ahead of them near to the corner of Demesne Street. She was travelling in the same direction as the bus which at the time was going at a steady pace.

Seconds later, the woman made a thoughtless decision to cross the road, totally oblivious to the oncoming traffic. Immediately realising the danger the driver called out to warn her, as did Thomas Stokes. At first she did not seem to hear, but on finally glancing back and seeing the bus Mrs Hepburn began to quicken her previously casual pace. The driver meanwhile was vigorously applying the brakes, but even so the vehicle was still going at about 6mph. In her haste the aged widow stumbled and fell flat on the ground. The driver desperately tried to halt the bus and at least steer around the woman. But it was too late. One of the heavy wheels rolled over Mrs Hepburn causing her weak and fragile body to sustain fatal injuries.

The bus continued to roll for a further 12yds before the driver and Mr Stokes could get off and come to Isabella's aid. Other passengers and a small group of passers-by also hurried over to offer their assistance. They found her lying on her back, her face gashed. It was not clear to them then that she had been killed.

The following day an inquest into the death of the sixty-five-year-old was

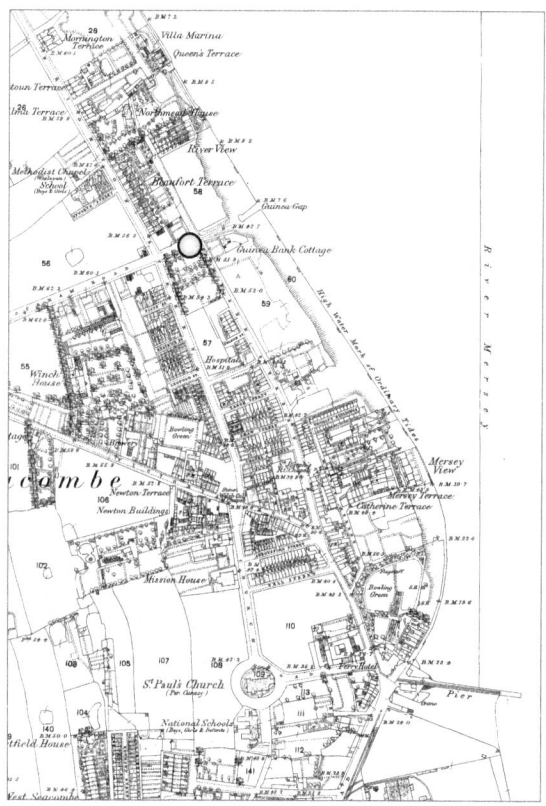

The corner of Brougham Road and Demesne Street on a map dated 1870.

The corner of Demesne Street, 2007.

held at the Stanley Arms Hotel, Seacombe. It was heard that the deceased was the widow of a sea captain and had lived in Coultard Road, Liverpool. She had been staying over in Liscard with some friends at a house in Cumberland Road and by all accounts she was a fit and healthy woman who had always been very firm on her feet.

Mr Moore, who appeared on behalf of the omnibus company, made it clear that the driver had pulled up as soon as he noticed the danger, but no earthly power could have stopped that bus in time. The witness pointed out that there was also a slight downward incline in the road, further preventing the driver from pulling up as soon as he otherwise would have done. Sadly it seemed if Mrs Hepburn had not had fallen over that terrible morning, she would not have been struck at all.

A verdict of accidental death was returned.

SAND SUFFOCATION

In 1909 a most shocking and gruesome discovery was made upon the picturesque sandhills of New Brighton. On the afternoon of 13 January, Thomas Clarke of Wallasey Village and his six-year-old son, Reggie, set out for a quiet walk along the cliff. As they made their way across the clifftop, Mr Clarke noticed that the landscape had changed slightly; the sand had moved. Reggie's inquisitive gaze was caught by something yet more peculiar. He peered closer. Just over the cliff the boy could see something dark and unusual sticking out of the dune. After a few moments Reggie's eyes were able to distinguish what the strange object was and immediately called out to his dad, 'There's a boy's boot!'

Father and son carefully made their way down to the sandhills to get a better look. On closer inspection they found that Reggie was right; it was a shoe and it was in

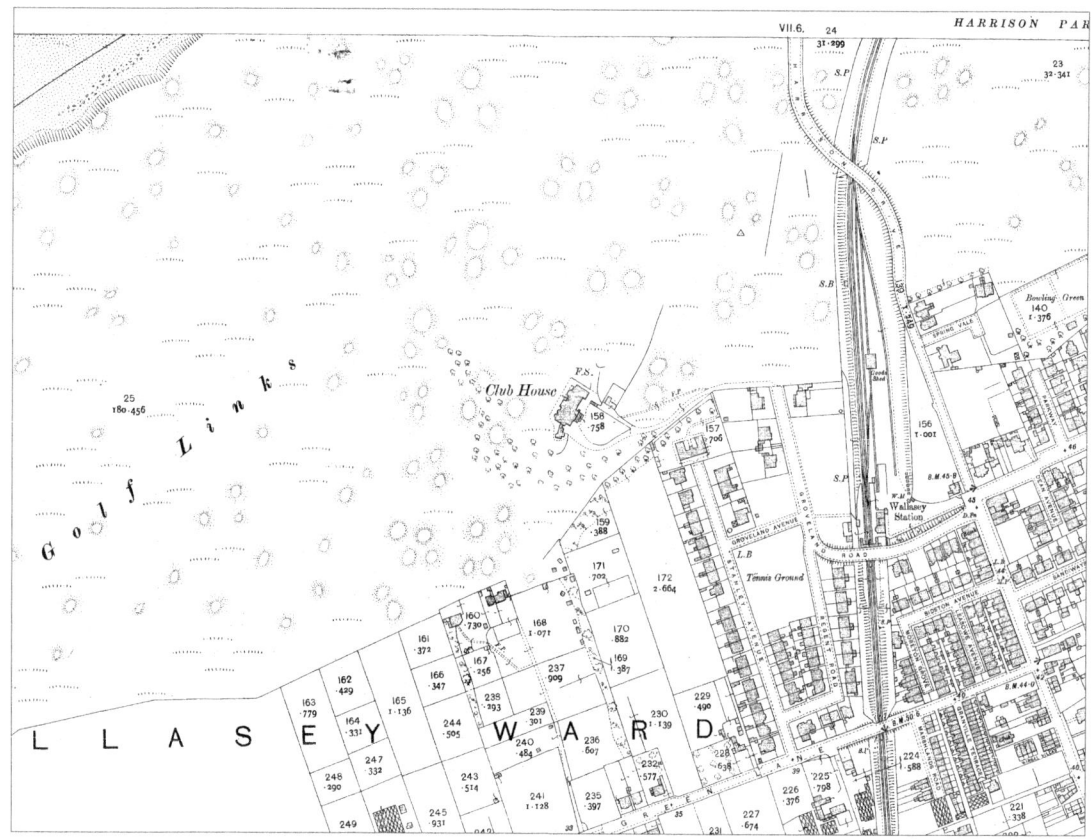

The vicinity of Wallasey Golf Club on a map dated 1912.

SAND SUFFOCATION

A view of Wallasey Golf Club from the course, c. 1900.

fact attached to a human leg. Mr Clarke suddenly recalled the terrible article that he had read in the paper. Fourteen-year-old Alfred Kemp had recently gone missing from his home at 36 Turret Road, Liscard. The boy had left his home on the previous Wednesday at about one-thirty with the intention of reading Walter Scott's *Quentin Durward* at his leisure. However, he had failed to return, creating the utmost alarm and leaving his family distraught. Since then there had been numerous searches over many hours, including the gallant efforts of 500 of Baden Powell's Boy Scouts, but none of these parties had yielded any results.

'Could this be the missing child?' Thomas thought to himself.

He told little Reggie to run across to the Wallasey Golf Club and ask for the police to be contacted on their telephone.

Superintendent McHale and his team were soon on the spot and quickly began digging about the protruding limb. Eventually, they were able work their way through 3ft of sand to recover the whole body. It was that of the missing boy. The manner in which his death was brought about was clear to all present. Alfred was lying stretched out on his right side, his left arm partially extended as if to ward off some impending danger. His cap sat on his head just as it did when he was alive, and in his pocket was his favourite book. It seemed that the youth had taken to sitting at the base of the dune to shield himself from a particularly strong wind. These sorts of winds were known to often cause violent and sudden shifts in the sand and that a large amount must have fallen from the overhanging edge, burying the poor lad instantly.

Wallasey Golf Club, 2007.

On 18 January an inquest was held by the West Cheshire Coroner, Mr J.C. Bate. A jury returned a verdict of accidental death by asphyxiation and many heartfelt condolences were expressed to the Kemp family.

CLOTHES COMBUSTION

Today we are constantly warned of the dangers of the modern household and information and advice regarding fire prevention are often passed on to us by the officers of local fire brigades. In 1913, such advice would have been well-heeded, as mother Mary Jane Williams found to her cost.

On Wednesday 15 October four-year-old Ivy Williams was sitting on the floor of the kitchen at her home at 59 Livingstone Street, Birkenhead. Her mother, Mary Jane, was busy preparing some washing as a small fire burned heating up the boiler. Just then, she realised that she would have to call round to a neighbour's house to borrow a mangle. In recent months the family had fallen on hard times, and Mary Jane had been forced to take in washing to keep the family home going. So, seeing that the boiler door was closed, and knowing that she would only be a few minutes at the most, Mary Jane left the property and walked briskly down the road in search of a mangle.

In the short time that she was away, young Ivy's curiosity got the better of her. Enticed by the flickering flames within, she wandered over to the boiler and opened

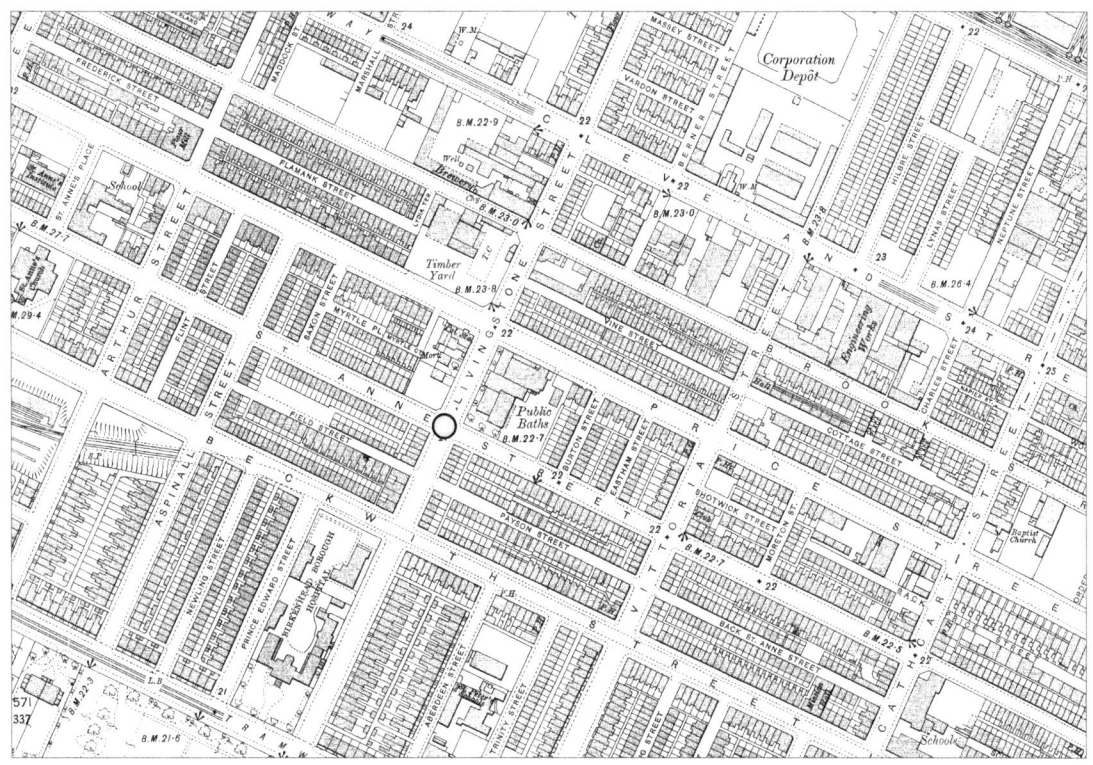

Livingstone Street, Birkenhead, from a map dated 1912.

A view of Livingstone Street, where young Ivy Williams was engulfed in flames in 1913.

the cover door. The little girl then proceeded to poke the fire with a stick that was lying nearby and watched as it began to singe. It was then that Ivy's latest source of entertainment turned against her. The poor girl's clothes ignited and soon Ivy was ablaze. Terrified, she ran through the house screaming for her mother, but she was nowhere to be seen.

Fifteen-year-old Jabez Hughes was passing the house as the orange ball of fire rushed out from the hallway. He at once took off his coat and began to suppress the scorching flames which had engulfed the toddler. The teenager successfully managed to extinguish the fire despite the very real danger that he himself would also catch light. He then carried Ivy to the Borough Hospital in Park Road North where she was treated by junior house surgeon Dr Brown. He found her to be suffering from severe shock and had sustained severe burns to her abdomen, arms and legs. Dr Brown also found parts of her face to be badly burnt. He knew she would not survive and at five o'clock the following morning, young Ivy Williams passed away.

At a subsequent inquest it was discovered that part of Ivy's clothing consisted of flannelette. The coroner questioned Mrs Williams about why she had dressed her child in such material.

'I knew flannelette was dangerous, but I have not read of any fatalities caused by it in the papers', Mary Jane responded.

In addressing the jury the coroner pointed out the danger of flannelette, remarking that it was a great pity that people persisted in purchasing it, seeing as there was a similar material available that was non-flammable.

The jury returned a verdict of accidental death and complimented Mr Hughes on his promptness in trying to save Ivy's life.

THE TUNNEL TOT

On the afternoon of 19 January 1891, Mrs Traynor, an artiste, stepped aboard the 1.45pm train from James Street, Liverpool, along with her two young children, the elder of whom she ushered maternally into the safety of the carriage. They were making the journey to Birkenhead to visit the Argyle Theatre in Argyle Street. The venue was famous for the quality of its performances, which over the years would feature stars such as Sir Harry Lauder, Vesta Tilley, Stan Laurel and Charlie Chaplin, to name but a few.

As the short journey commenced, Mrs Traynor became preoccupied as she rocked her crying baby to her shoulder. The little one craved attention and Mrs Traynor lovingly obliged. With all her focus centred on her youngest child, the woman failed to notice her four-year-old toddler merrily playing with the carriage door handle.

Soon the five-minute journey neared its end and the passengers aboard prepared to alight from the train. Just then the curious Traynor toddler managed to turn the handle fully, causing the door to fly open. A howling wind swept throughout the whole carriage and papers blew about wildly as a chill rushed in from the dark underground passage. Mrs Traynor's blood turned to ice as she looked out to see her elder child fall onto the lines and become an indistinguishable shadow in the distance. In a matter of seconds the train arrived at Hamilton Square and the brakes screeched to a shuddering halt. Mrs Traynor flung her baby into the arms of a complete stranger and jumped onto the track.

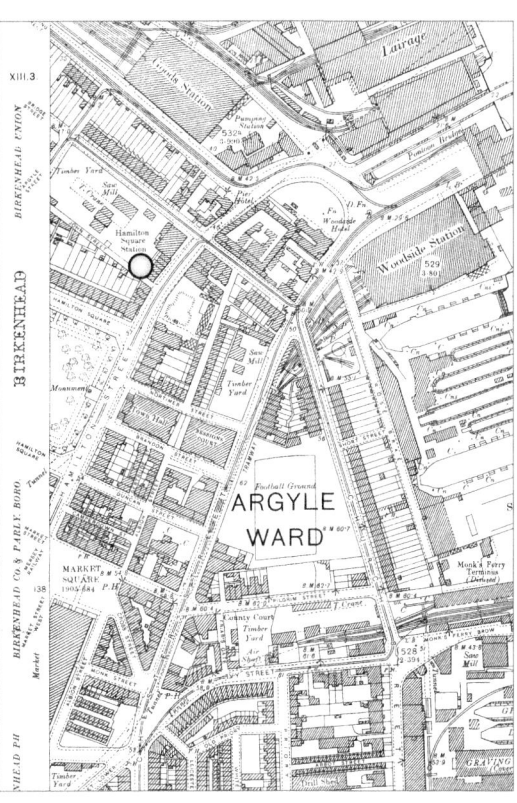

Hamilton Square station, taken from a map dated 1898.

'My child has fallen onto the lines!' she screamed, as she fled down the tunnel. On the platform, Inspector Burge ran intrepidly to the signal-box and at once ordered the stopping of the 1.50pm train from Liverpool. Across the water the locomotive had already collected its passengers and was only moments away from

Hamilton Square station in the early twentieth century.

departing. It was then that the signals were set to 'danger' and the impending catastrophe was averted.

With the track made sufficiently safe, a search party set off down the tunnel after Mrs Traynor to rescue the lost tot. A few fearful moments later they returned from the darkness clutching the frightened child whom they found several yards down the line. Incredibly the child had sustained no serious injuries and seemed perfectly happy once in the arms of its caring mother, who would no doubt go on to keep a much closer eye on both of her children in the future.

OBSERVATORY PLUMMET

On the afternoon of Thursday 21 April 1892 an inquest into the death of renowned Wirral astronomer, fifty-one year-old John Hartnup, was formally opened. In 1888, twenty-five years after the Liverpool Observatory had relocated to Bidston Hill, John Hartnup Snr retired and was succeeded by his son as director. John Hartnup Jnr, educated at the Royal Institution School, Liverpool, and later at a private academy in Chester, was appointed as his father's assistant at the age of twenty-one. Over the years he continued to develop his father's pioneering studies of chronometers and often gave advice to the United States Naval Observatory in Washington regarding his studies.

As astronomer to the Mersey Docks and Harbour Board, it was part of Mr Hartnup's duties to inspect from time to time, both day and night, the anemometers. These instruments automatically registered the direction and force of the wind. This was achieved through a set of scientific devices positioned on the observatory roof, and to ensure accuracy they were required to be examined at regular intervals.

Earlier on that April morning, between six and seven o'clock, Mr Hartnup went to the roof to check the fan-wheels. He was with his sister-in-law, Miss Hammond, who made her way up the stairs to join him. As she climbed the stairs she spotted Hartnup near to the guard wall. He was looking upwards, to inspect the anemometers which stood between the two telescopic domes. Continuing her ascent, Miss Hammond watched aghast as Mr Hartnup stumbled backwards and called out, before disappearing out of sight over the wall. She ran up the remaining stairs and looked over to see his body lying on the gravel path below. Dr Harris was called for, but Mr Hartnup was already dead; his neck having been broken. Death had been instantaneous.

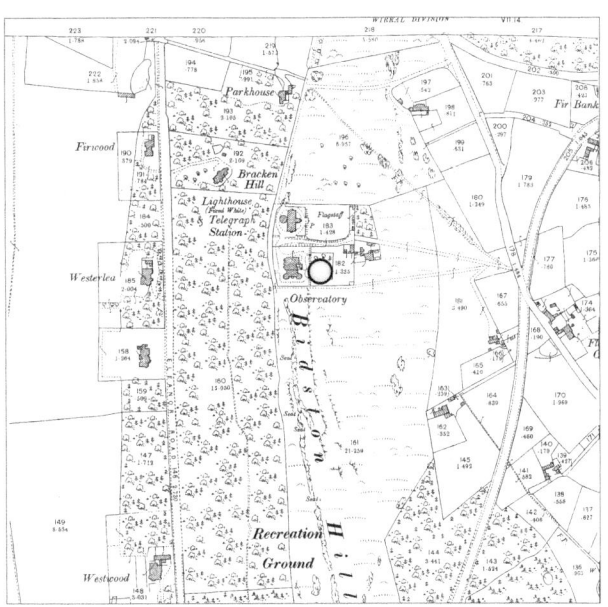

Bidston Hill on a map dating from 1898.

A Victorian view of Bidston Observatory.

At the inquest, Miss Hammond stated that only fifteen minutes before Mr Hartnup's untimely demise she had spoken with him and he seemed in perfect health. However she did mention that her brother-in-law had recently been troubled by periods of giddiness, but had not spoken to a doctor about them, believing they would pass soon enough.

'I suppose these attacks of giddiness come on very suddenly?' asked the coroner.

'Yes. On Tuesday last, whilst out for a drive, an attack came on and I had to bring him home by train: Otherwise he was a perfectly healthy looking man. I saw him immediately after he fell, and I think he must have been killed on the spot.' Miss Hammond replied.

It was heard that the wall over which the deceased fell was a mere 20in high. Mr Hartnup often warned friends and family not to stray too close to the edge whenever they came to visit. The jury returned a verdict of accidental death and added that the wall was too low for the purpose for which it was built. They put a strong recommendation to the Dock Board to have the wall supervised and heightened, with the view of affording full protection to anyone in the future.

At the meeting of the Mersey Docks and Harbour Board later that day, the chairman made an appreciative and sympathetic reference to Mr Hartnup's lifelong dedication to his profession and his sad fate.

MUNITIONS MAINTENANCE

In 1890, thirty-five-year-old adventurer Henry Sproston Hall returned to his home, Larchwood, in Kings Lane, Higher Bebington. He had been abroad seeing the world and had only recently returned to the Wirral after an absence of about two years.

On the wintry afternoon of 27 December, Henry was in the harness room of the house cleaning his guns. With him was John Flanagan, coachman to Henry's father. John would often volunteer to clean his master's firearms but on this occasion Henry chose to do it himself and refused the kind offer from the faithful family servant.

'Never mind, I quite like the job', Henry chuckled.

Mr Hall proceeded to remove the dirt and grime from the weapon and with a spot of elbow grease the gun was as good as new.

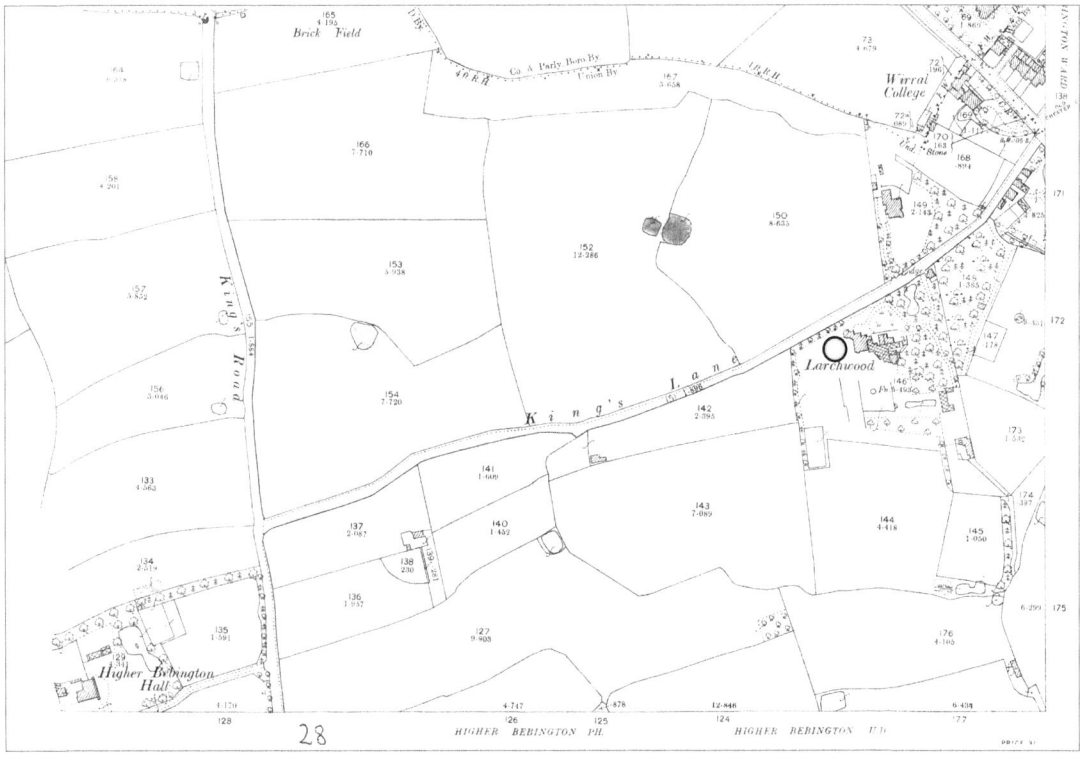

Larchwood in Kings Lane, Bebington, from a map dated 1899.

'We will have a go at this', Hall said proudly, as his gaze turned to his next task. He picked up a second gun, a five-chambered revolver known as an American Bulldog, a small hand-held weapon with a long silver barrel. He began to remove two of the cartridges from the chamber before taking a seat to extract a third. It was proving to be a somewhat difficult undertaking and Henry's face registered a look of annoyance as he fiddled irritably with the cumbersome weapon. At this point the trusty coachman left to hang up his coat on the wall, leaving his master to attend to the gun alone. While his back was turned, John heard a loud crack before hearing Mr Hall let out an almighty groan. Flanagan immediately turned to face his master.

'Oh my God Mr Henry, what's the matter?' John exclaimed as he sped to Henry's side.

'I've been trying to clean the revolver', he whimpered. 'Lay me down on the floor. Send for a doctor!'

The coachman carefully aided Mr Hall to the ground and made him as comfortable as he could. On the floor John noticed the revolver's bolt had been blown separate from the main unit. This led him to infer that the gun must have accidentally exploded while Mr Hall was trying to withdraw it.

'Get my mother and father', he pleaded. Mr Flanagan hurried into the main building and informed Mr Hall Snr and his wife of the accident. Upon hearing the news the elderly couple enlisted the help of their gardener and hurried into the harness room. Between them, they escorted Henry outside and led him up to his private bedroom. 'What a beautiful day it is. I would have liked to have attended the meet of the Beagles', Henry commented, seemingly unaware of the dangerous predicament his life was now in. Leaving Henry with his family, the coachman quickly exited the house in search of professional help. He found Dr Carruthers, a Rock Ferry surgeon, and urged him to attend to the injured man at Larchwood. At about one o'clock the doctor arrived at the house and made for Henry's bedroom. To his surprise he found the patient standing, partially dressed. From what he had been told the surgeon expected Mr Hall to be lying stricken in his bed, but nevertheless the doctor greeted the man and proceeded to examine him. On inspection Dr Carruthers discovered that Henry had sustained a small wound to the lower part of his breast bone. He also noticed a slight oozing of blood and remarked that Mr Hall was looking a little pale. Henry told him that he did not feel too well and that he felt anxious and rather faint. These symptoms set off alarm bells in the doctor's medical mind; he at once suspected the possibility of internal haemorrhaging. He conducted a closer inspection and on doing so located extensive internal bleeding. Dr Carruthers battled fervently to avert further blood loss. The bullet could not be retrieved and the wound would not coagulate. The unseen bleeding persisted until Henry died. The doctor did everything that could possibly have been done, but regrettably his best efforts were not enough.

An inquest into the fatality was held on 5 January 1891 by Dr Churton. Great sympathy was expressed to the Hall family, with wishes that they would be divinely sustained during their dark hour. A verdict of accidental death was returned.

OUT FOR THE COUNT

On the afternoon of 18 June 1909, Joshua Hunt, a twenty-six-year-old butcher, visited the Feathers Inn, a pub owned by John Nesbitt, in Chester Street, Birkenhead. He was with some friends all of whom ordered their drinks before engaging in some light-hearted banter. Upon hearing the joviality Thomas Brooks, the landlord's twenty-two-year-old stepson, joined the party and was soon laughing and joking along with the crowd. Eventually the conversation turned to boxing. On a previous visit to the pub Thomas, who was well acquainted with the regulars, had challenged Joshua to a friendly match at the nearby boxing club. Joshua had declined the offer, but now Thomas challenged him once again.

'Are you of the same principle as previously? Come to the drill shed and have a spar', Brooks cajoled, and he bet Joshua the sum of 10s. This time the butcher gave in and agreed to an affable bout later that afternoon. Shortly afterwards Brooks left the pub and made his way to the Denbigh Castle pub where he informed some friends of the forthcoming fight. Harold McKeller overheard the news. He was the brother of Walter McKeller, proprietor of the boxing hall in Priory Street. He joined

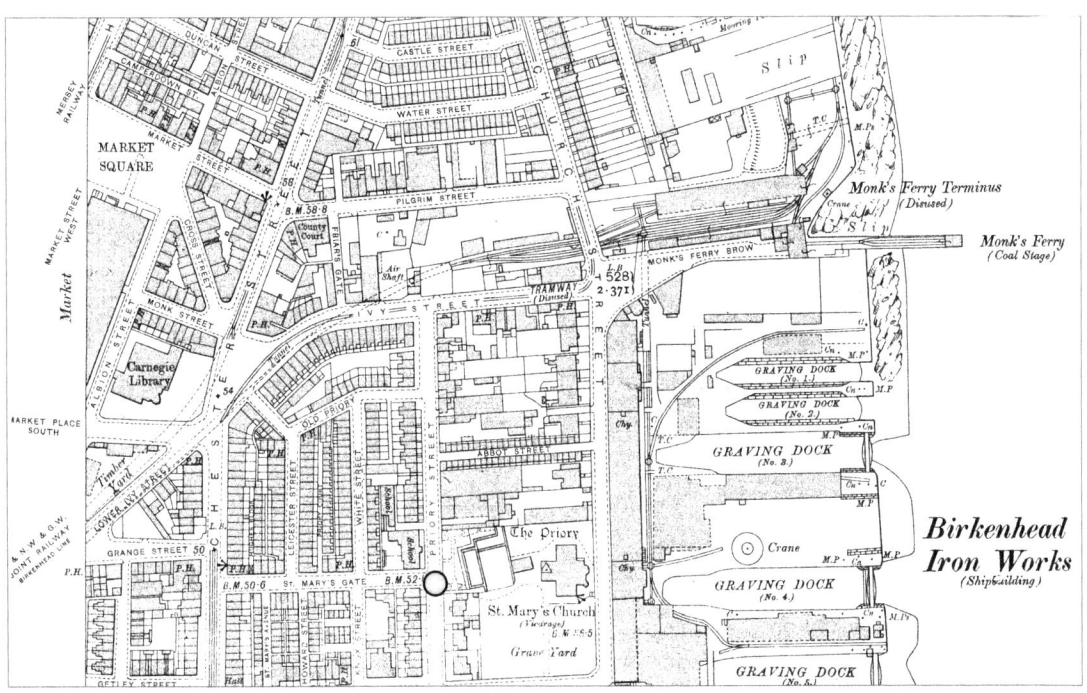

Priory Street on a map dated 1911.

the conversation whereupon he was asked if he would be willing to referee the match. Harold nodded and at about 4.30pm, he followed Thomas and his friends out of the pub and over into the hall.

Joshua Hunt arrived shortly after and made his way to the ring. The two contenders took off their coats and waistcoats; Hunt also opting to remove his shirt.

'Don't hurt me too much!', the butcher said with a nervous grin. He had never been in such a situation and was feeling rather anxious at the ever-increasing number of spectators.

Neither of the men was very fit; Brooks being quite the heavyweight weighing in at about 16st, with Hunt tipping the scales at a more modest 11st. Nevertheless, McKeller obtained two pairs of gloves, about eight ounces in weight, before dictating the rules. He told them that they must fight fairly, and that no clinching would be tolerated. The rounds were to last two minutes each with one-minute intervals and this was by no means a fight to the finish. The winner would be decided upon points. A man named Thomas Whelligan, a local hairdresser, was selected as Brooks's second and another spectator was chosen for Hunt. By this time the hall had filled with about forty people all eager to see the amateur bout. Thomas Lawton acted as timekeeper and on his shout the fight got underway.

'Give it to the winner!' a voice shouted from the crowd and a sovereign rolled into the ring. McKeller retrieved it and stepped aside. The fight would now commence.

In the first round both men were eager to land the first punch. With about six or seven strikes between them, mostly about the arms and shoulders, both competitors seemed equal as their vigour carried them tumbling through the ropes.

Both men prepared to fight once again. They climbed back into their respective corners and waited on McKeller's word. Several uneventful rounds followed with no man gaining the upper hand, both only losing breath.

By round five, and despite a short interval, exhaustion had taken hold of both Thomas and Joshua and both men were struggling to muster strength.

Soon enough it was time to duel again. Fearing total fatigue was a mere moment away, Brooks made a sudden rush at Hunt in a final attempt to win the match. But Hunt was too fast and stepped aside, sending the plump electrician plummeting through the ropes once again. Brooks crashed into a bench before rolling inelegantly to the ground as the crowd jeered with distasteful delight.

McKeller jumped down from the ring to see whether Brooks was injured.

'I'm alright. It is only my wind. I am troubled with my wind a bit', Thomas answered breathlessly. He told the amateur adjudicator that he wished to continue with the fight. He would be well again in a few minutes. His second, Thomas Whelligan, shook his head despondently and informed him that the match was over. There was no way he could continue in such a shattered state. Hunt had won. Joshua was given the prize sovereign and enjoyed hearty applause from the gathering of onlookers.

Tom Brooks on the other hand had gone into the adjoining yard with Hunt and McKeller for some air, but his exhaustion seemed to be getting worse.

Priory Street, where the fatal bout took place, as it looks in 2007.

The lessee, Walter McKeller, arrived at the club and upon seeing the defeated man's increasingly poorly condition gave him some brandy before sending for a cab to return him home. On his return, Brooks' health continued to worsen and by six o'clock he was dead.

Dr Wilkinson was sent for and immediately pronounced life extinct. He contacted PC Crawshaw who, together with Inspector Bebbington and Superintendent Parker, investigated the case.

An inquest into the death was held before the Borough Coroner on the morning of Monday 23 June. From the evidence given to him by those present at the hall and by doctors Wilkinson and Preece, it was clear that the deceased had died from exhaustion. At the post-mortem there were no signs of any external injury, but it was obvious to the doctors that Thomas Brooks had been unfit to have engaged safely in any form of strenuous exercise. The two rivals were perfectly sober and had begun, and ended, the fight on good terms, so there could be no blame attributed to Joshua Hunt. Therefore it was agreed that death was due to exhaustion consequent of heart failure.

The coroner further stated that the police did not wish to stop legitimate amusement of this sort, but it was clear that individuals such as Brooks, in regards to training, should never be allowed to fight in such a haphazard manner in the hall. He told Mr McKeller that he would be well advised to have proper supervision in the hall in future, so that regrettable incidents such as this could be avoided.

'It will never occur again', McKeller solemnly replied.

A WOEFUL WASH

On 3 February 1908 the Batchelor family of 80 Willmer Road, Tranmere, suffered a tremendous loss. That morning Annie Batchelor, wife of PC George Batchelor, was at the terraced house with her one-month-old baby daughter, Hilda. Annie had only recently recovered from an illness and had been forced to take a break from her housework chores for the past fourteen days. During her period of rest, Mrs Batchelor had suffered an unexpected fainting fit in the kitchen. Luckily her husband was at home at the time and prevented any unfortunate injuries. However, after a fortnight of recovery, Annie was now feeling much better, but still felt slightly weak. Earlier that morning she had complained of feeling a little dizzy, but the sensation soon passed and Mrs Batchelor carried on her work about the house. At about ten-thirty, she made her way into the kitchen in preparation for bathing baby Hilda. She prepared a zinc bath and carefully filled the tub three-quarters full of warm water before testing the temperature with her elbow.

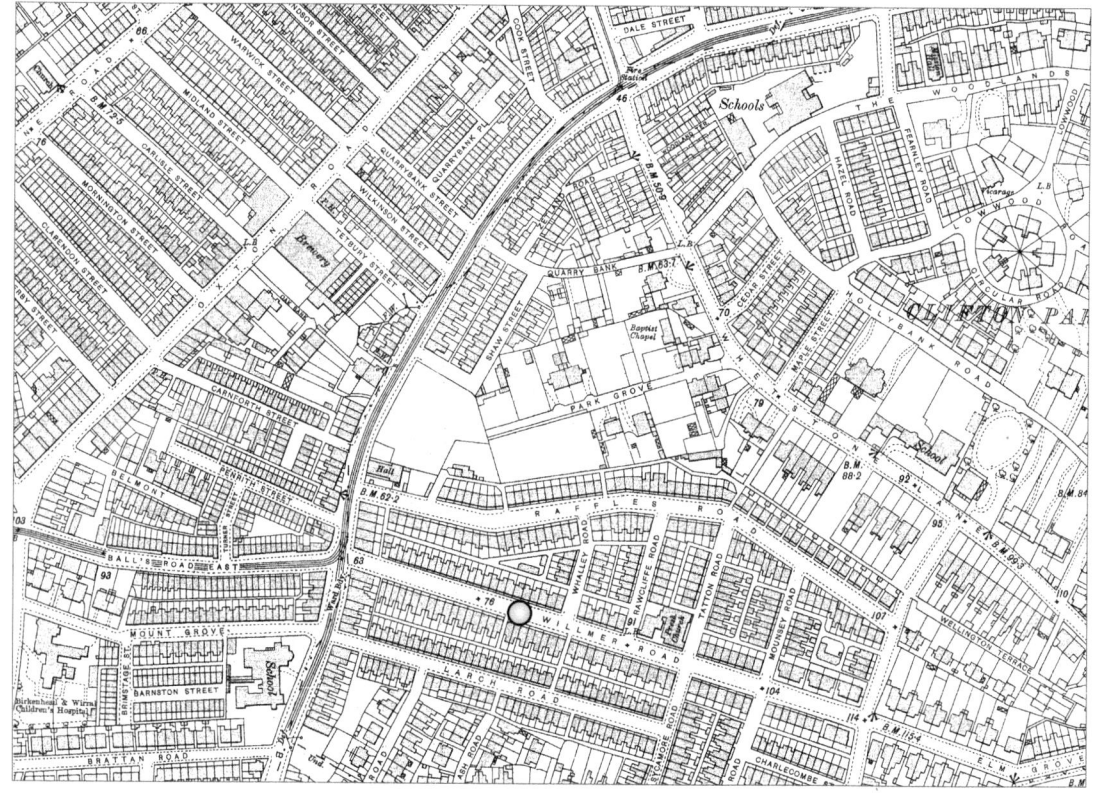

Willmer Road on a map from 1911.

Willmer Road, 2007.

With the water ready, Annie collected her daughter and undressed her, before carrying the baby over to the bath. With her free arm she reached up to the clothes line that stretched high across the room in order to grab a towel for drying. Suddenly Annie felt uneasy and the poor woman lost her balance before fainting on the hard kitchen floor. After several moments, Annie awoke. Upon standing and regaining her composure, she was horrified to discover her baby lying at the bottom of the bath. In a state of utter panic Annie ran upstairs to get her own mother, Mrs Young, who at once hurried down the narrow staircase to see what on earth the matter was. In the metallic container which sat in the centre of the room, lay the lifeless body of her newborn granddaughter. Mrs Young gently picked the dripping corpse from the water and laid it on the floor. She then hurried out of the house in search of a doctor.

Dr J. Dixon was found. He had been Mrs Batchelor's attendant while she had been ill and was well-acquainted with the family. He listened to Mrs Young's sorrowful plight before immediately rushing to the property in Willmer Road where he examined the tot. Sadly, there was nothing he could do. Hilda had drowned.

A post-mortem later confirmed that the child tragically died from asphyxiation consequent of immersion. It was said that Mrs Batchelor's fainting episodes were most likely to have been brought about through stress. The resumption of housework a little too early no doubt contributed to her blackouts. Annie was a most careful and attentive parent whose grave misfortunate warranted the most sincere sympathy from across the borough.

A MUNICIPAL MISFORTUNE

The splendid summer evening of 10 July 1901 was the setting for the annual conference of the British Association of Waterworks Engineers. This fine event was held at the borough's majestic Town Hall set in the heart of the blossoming Hamilton Square. At about nine o'clock, Mr Richardson, the president of the association, had proposed two royal toasts; 'The health of the Mayor and Corporation of Birkenhead', he cheered. All was going pleasantly; dinner was over and the vocal quartet had performed several pieces for the crowd's entertainment.

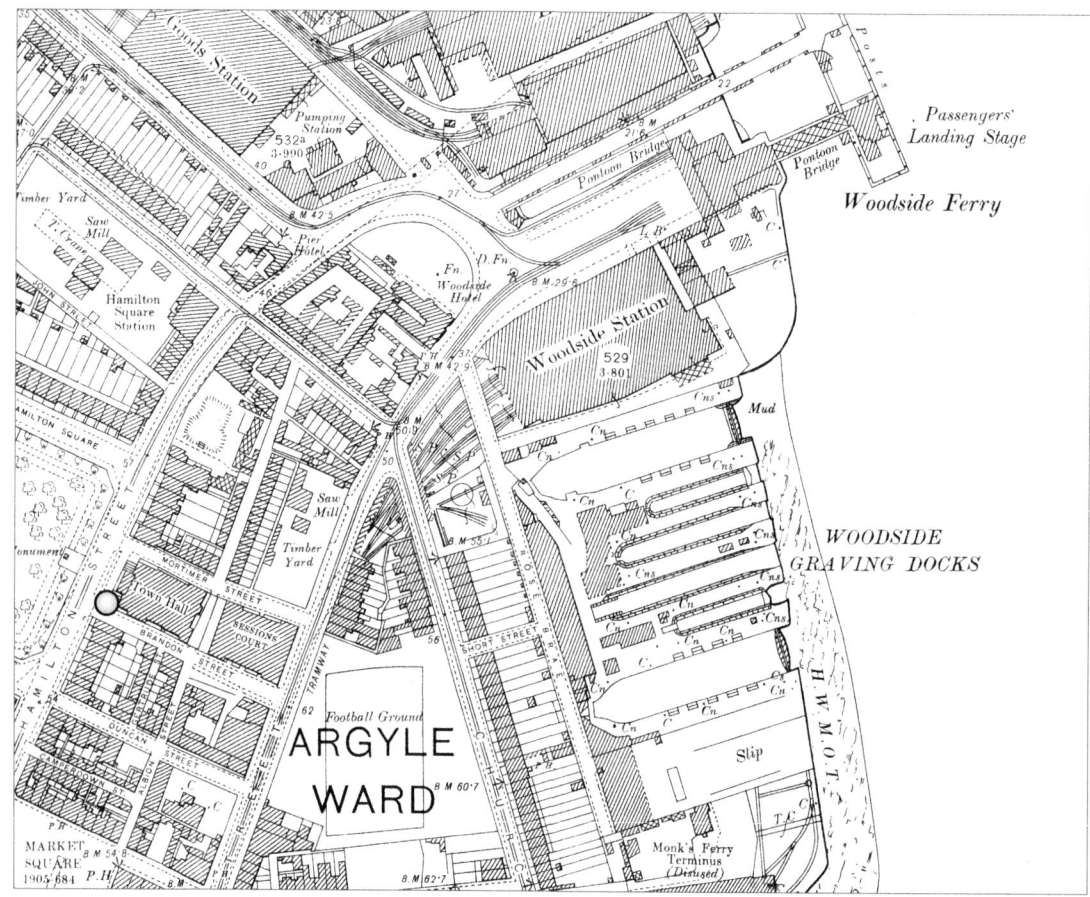

The Town Hall on a map dating from 1899.

At about quarter-past nine the musicians were performing a calming love song, much to the delight of the fifty or so distinguished guests who were feeling rather full from their meals and wine. It was then that some dreadful commotion began to drown out the singers' voices. The waiters peered out of the windows and a small number of inquisitive guests, one by one, got up from their seats and followed.

'The Town Hall's afire!' was the ominous cry. The singers fell silent and soon the guests rushed back into the main dining area to pass on the terrible news to those who had failed to heed the cries. Nevertheless, the majority of the attendees gave the tale no credit and continued to chat and gossip.

The secretary of the waterworks came over to the Mayor Alderman Thomas Cook.

'I don't want to cause any alarm or excitement, but I am sorry to say that the roof of the Town Hall is on fire'. Before this warning the secretary had spoken quietly to another guest, Chief Constable Davies, who had already vacated the room to help organise a salvage operation. The mayor quietly got up from his seat and walked calmly with Mr Richardson to see whether this, seemingly implausible, information was true. Sure enough he was amazed to see the orange flames issuing from the ante-room. The magnificent chandelier, which hung ceremoniously from the ceiling, was already ablaze. On the staircase stood the impeccably dressed Chief Constable, bravely tackling the blaze with the emergency hosepipe. At ground level were Mr Bates, the head electrical engineer, and a small band of eagle-eyed diners who were using small hand pumps and buckets to help quell the flames.

Despite his racing pulse, the mayor returned coolly to his seat, keen not to cause any panic; the makeshift firefighters would soon have control of the situation.

However not long afterwards word of the conflagration leaked out and the lavish evening was quickly drawn to a halt. A handful of guests began to remove the expensive oil paintings which adorned the walls. The large portrait of John Laird was so firmly secured that it had to be forcibly torn away from its framework before being carried out to the safety of the neighbouring police station.

Superintendent Smith of the Borough Fire Brigade was contacted and in a matter of minutes he was on the scene with his brigade. A ladder was positioned sturdily up against the Brandon Street side of the building and immediately a hose was attached to a street hydrant and forced through to spray upon the roof, which was now a truly ferocious sight. The fire had a firm hold, and clouds of black smoke billowed high into the evening sky. The gas was ordered to be switched off and firemen raced into the ante-room. They assisted the Chief Constable and Mr Roberts, the hall keeper, both of whom in ascending the narrow staircase to the roof space were so much overcome by burning vapours that they had to be escorted down.

By nine-forty the roof of the ante-room on the Mortimer Street front corner was well ablaze and it appeared that the Council Chamber would soon suffer a similar fate.

Only five minutes later the fire had made considerable progress and engulfed the 200ft high Town Hall tower. It burst into a single torch-like illumination. Fiery timbers began to break away, putting the valiant firemen in the square at considerable risk. They moved back and began to focus their efforts on saving the main buildings and the base of the tower. The four-faced clock on which it stood was so furiously alight that it seemed a waste of labour even to attempt to save it. Indeed, Superintendent Smith knew that extinguishing the flames at the pinnacle would have sent the fire into the belfry. Had that become ablaze, the monumental bells would have become hazardous and possibly have collapsed, falling through and dismantling the main staircase, putting the whole building at risk

At ten the bells chimed, the glass of the clockface reflecting the captivating light which had created such a wonderful yet tragic spectacle. Word had spread across the town and Hamilton Square rapidly became a densely packed arena, the crowds cheering as the reverberating chimes rang out defiantly. Suddenly, the once-punctual minute finger fell helplessly to the ground and soon the bells took on a somewhat different tune. No longer did they sing boldly, but suffered a painful change of intonation. Now it cried dismal notes of sorrow, no doubt reflecting the feelings of all those who heard it. 'Good old bells', some cheered, 'poor old bells', said others.

A little after ten the clock surrendered to the heat and finally stopped ticking. The end was near, but still the number of spectators increased. Crowds congregated and lined the streets with avid interest. Argyle Street South, Holt Hill and Church Road gave curious locals the best vantage points. The trams of New Ferry were besieged as neighbouring residents flocked to the town for free entertainment. Seats were soon full, forcing New Chester Road to become a hectic thoroughfare as masses of citizens walked to Birkenhead, their visages lit up by the marvellous glow.

Liverpool's landing stage bore the brunt of a multitude of cross-river watchers, whose unique view was beautifully magnified once darkness had descended. Yet many were not satisfied by this distant vantage point, opting to pack the ferries and travel across the Mersey for a closer look. The turbulent glare of the Town Hall catastrophe could be seen from as far away as Everton and Toxteth.

Firefighters continued valiantly in their efforts, but by half-past ten the inevitable took place. The tower framework, disabled by pressure, buckled, causing the imposing structure to fall through an array of luxuriously-decorated rooms amid a radiant shower of sparks. Bystanders could do nothing but look on in amazement as the glowing beacon that had once stood so fantastically before them plunged into what appeared to be a mortar-clad abyss.

Gasps could be heard all around as the enthralling display of accidental might came to a crashing end. Soon after, the throngs of locals began to disperse, clearing the once-heaving streets of Brandon, Mortimer, Duncan and Hamilton. Few stayed to watch the Thursday morning clear-up operation, but those who did witnessed two further accidents. One fireman sustained an electric shock while working on the rooftop and was sent plummeting to the ground. Remarkably he suffered no injury and was hauled up by a rope to continue his duties. His colleague, fireman John Denson, sustained a more serious injury. He was working on the remains of the tower when part of the iron framework fell and punctured his leg, greatly bruising the other. An ambulance was sent for and he was conveyed to the Borough Hospital.

Birkenhead Town Hall before the terrible fire of 1901.

By daybreak the fire had been successfully extinguished, but a number of rooms had paid a costly price. Superintendent Smith's careful planning, wisdom and professional organisation skills contributed significantly to the successful avoidance of any greater disaster or loss of life.

In the cold light of day the true toll of the night's events became apparent to all. A chaotic scene of desolation and ruin lay behind the heavy front doors that adorned the once noble building. On climbing the stone steps, rolled-up carpets, still dripping with water, were the first indication of the previous night's drama; they reclined weeping in the portico. Walking inside and passing through to the Borough Treasurer's suite witnesses observed a most melancholy picture. Water was still raining down from the ornate but saturated ceilings, broken debris lay about the sodden floor space and lines of desks glistened in their soaked state. The Town Clerk's department offered a similar perspective, as did the Gas department, whose library suffered extensive water damage. The condition of the grand staircase and its corridor showed indisputable evidence of the vast deluge of water that had flowed down it like an indoor waterfall. Despite this, the damage in this part of the hall was not so terrible. The large impressive mirror which hung opposite the drenched staircase luckily had remained undamaged, but this could not be said for a once-handsome stained-glass window, which now bore a gaping hole. At the turn of the landing there was yet more debris, and upon entering the scene of the outbreak of the fire, the ante-room to the Council Chamber, it could be seen that the damage done to this room was most lamentable. Half of the ceiling had broken away and fallen into a sorry heap. As they gazed upwards, a giant yawning gulf, charred black at the edges, met the eyes of dismayed observers. Soot-laden rafters threatened to fly down at a moment's notice as they hung perilously above the heads of those charged with clearing the awful scene of devastation. In the stately Council Chamber the damage had been relatively light, but it was still enough. The delicate masonry and exquisite effect of stained-glass in the centre of the ceiling was now riddled with holes. In the Mayor's parlour the constant drip of water could not fail to be heard as damp paper clung feebly to the waterlogged walls. In the disintegrated tower the sturdy oak beams on which the bells hung, and upon which the Hall's future relied, had withstood the catastrophe to a surprising degree; they were not even charred.

The generally accepted theory of what had caused such a devastating occurrence was the unfortunate fusing of a wire in an ante-room electrolier. However, Mr Bates, the electrical engineer disputed this. He believed that if indeed the tragedy was caused by a chance fusing, then the thin electrical wires would have broken. He found these to be still intact and hanging from the electrolier. Despite his professional opinion no further investigations were made.

In consequence, all meetings due to take place at the Town Hall were postponed or forced to be held elsewhere. It was estimated that the restoration of the damaged rooms would take about six months to complete and the cost to replace the lost tower was to be an enormous £15,000.

A GUILTY PORTER

The terrible death of infant William Scholes was one that may have been avoided if it were not for the cold-hearted nature of a certain Borough Hospital porter. On 10 April 1876 three-year-old William was at his home when he accidentally caught alight. His mother, who was fetching water from the backyard at the time, hurried in and, with the help of a neighbour, extinguished the flames. However the front of the child's torso had suffered most appallingly. Mrs Scholes hailed a cab and at once rushed the child to the Borough Hospital in Park Road North. On arrival she and her neighbour rushed in, carrying the screaming youngster to the reception room. She found a porter and, frantic with worry, told him of the dreadful nature and urgency of the child's case.

'You'll have to wait your turn', he calmly told her, with no apparent comprehension that the toddler before him was slowly dying in his mother's arms. Mrs Scholes was kept waiting for a further three-quarters of an hour before the

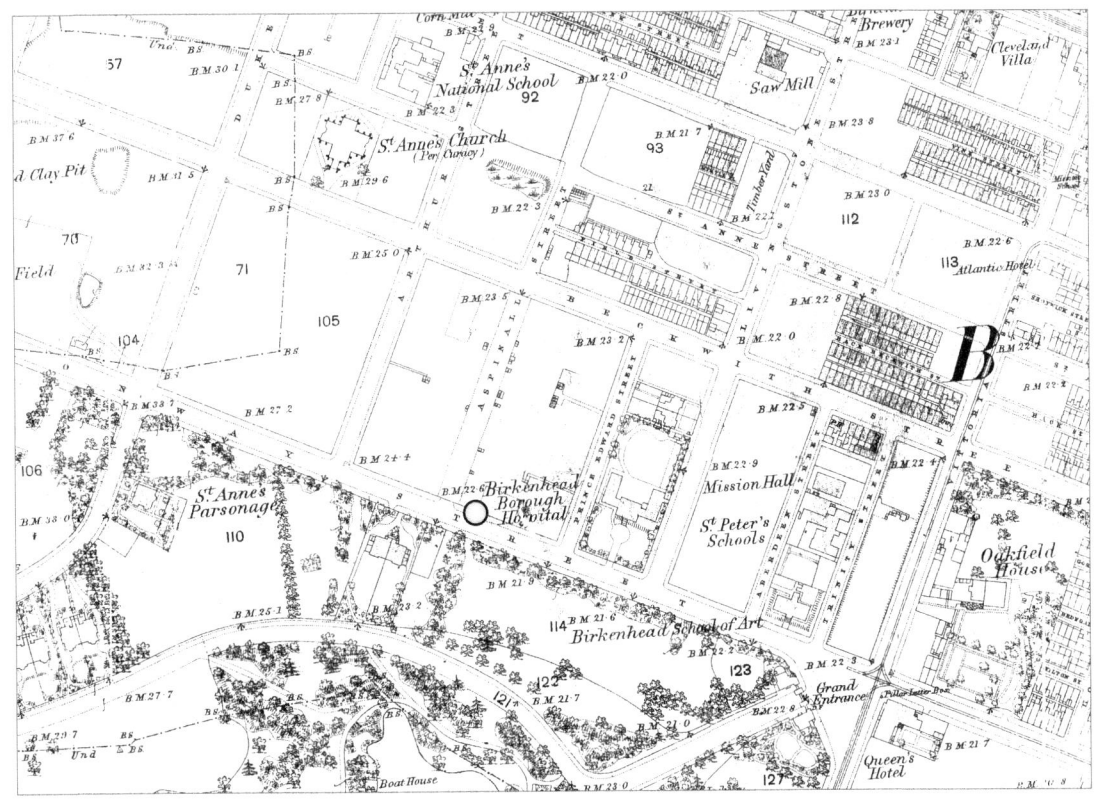

The Birkenhead Borough Hospital on a map dating from 1870.

The Borough Hospital, c. 1904.

constant and unbearable cries induced the porter to fetch the medical officer. On his arrival the officer promptly dressed the child's wounds and applied oil and cotton wool; a quantity of which he supplied to Mrs Scholes for later use. She then took William home.

Next morning William's fragile body could withstand the pain no longer, and he passed away.

An inquest held on the following Thursday highlighted the callous conduct of the porter responsible for ignoring Mrs Scholes' frantic pleas. The coroner was adamant that he would be informing the Hospital Committee in due course. They would no doubt take a keen interest in investigating such repugnant conduct in what was usually so excellent an institution.

A further revelation came to light when it was heard the same porter had acted with equal negligence only three days before the unnecessary death of the boy Scholes. Then, a child had been brought into the hospital suffering from a severe fit. The porter permitted the child to remain struggling in the waiting room for a whole twenty minutes before summoning the medical officer. On his arrival the child was already dead. Two verdicts of accidental death were recorded, with a presentment that the hospital employee was most culpable in not having sooner informed the house surgeon, Mr Cretin, of the urgency of the matters.

THE CALAMITY CRUISE

On 11 August 1895 an inquest was held into the deaths of three young Wirral men whose ill-fated maritime adventure led to their aqueous demise. On the morning of Saturday 9 August brothers Thomas and Phillip Bell and their two friends Frederick Campbell and George Ferguson met up at Tranmere Ferry with the intention setting off on a pleasure cruise around the peninsula. All four friends had had some experience out at sea and all were capable swimmers. They enthusiastically clambered aboard a yacht moored on the bank side and set sail for Hoylake. The vessel, which was large enough to seat six to eight people, allowed the men on board ample room to sit back and take in the stunning views of the huge sailing ships navigating their course across the Mersey. As they left Tranmere the river was calm and the waves were slight. With such little breeze, the group could do nothing but sit and wait for the wind to pick up. After about two hours, the sails began to flutter and sure enough the yacht was moving once again. Eventually the

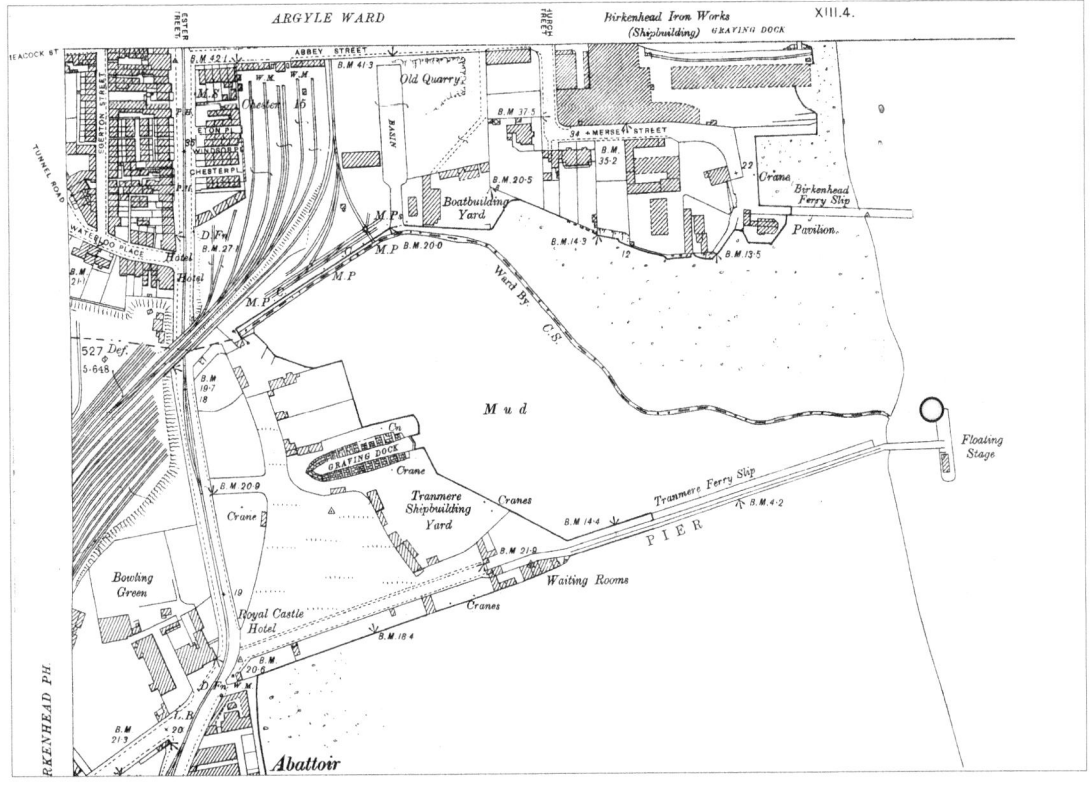

Tranmere Ferry on a map dating from 1899.

yachters were sailing competently around the peninsula, steering themselves near to Hilbre Island off the coast of West Kirby. With the wind now blowing harder than expected towards the shore, they ran aground near Hoyle Bank. The young men were forced to lower the sail and make use of the wooden oars to push the yacht back out into the estuary. Once successfully away from land the friends sailed down the bank hoping either to get over or around it. To their dismay they found that the bank gave a sharp turn right out to sea. They had no choice but to stay on course and travel out far from shore. By this time the wind had freshened and was blowing hard from the north-west, causing violent waves to crash fiercely against the vessel. After sailing out to a distance of 2 miles it was decided to try and turn the yacht round and head back to land. They prepared to come about, but in doing so the yacht capsized. George was thrown overboard, but his three friends managed to keep a hold. When he came to the surface George found he had been flung a whole 10yds from the boat. He took off his mackintosh coat and swam hastily back to the upturned craft. He and Frederick held the stern, while Phillip dived underneath the vessel and desperately cut the mast. The yacht suddenly righted itself, but with each crash the waves overturned her once again, thus yielding to a constant state of revolution. George held on tightly to one end of the boat, Thomas Bell had a grasp of the other and his brother was clutching tightly onto the top. There was neither land nor boat in sight and soon George slipped into unconsciousness. At about eight o'clock he recovered and found himself lying at the bottom of a rescue boat. He could neither recall how he had arrived there nor had he any recollection regarding the fate of his companions. The young man discovered that his pocket watch had ceased to work at twenty minutes past four, but how long he had been in the water was a mystery. His rescuer gave him some rum and after about half an hour George was able to relate his final memories of that fateful afternoon. After listening to his harrowing account the boatman described how he had himself found George clinging unconscious to the boat. He had seen no sign of George's three friends.

The bodies of two of the men were later found. That of Frederick Campbell was discovered floating off Crosby by a fisherman and a Board of Trade representative, who immediately towed the corpse back to shore. The body of Phillip Bell was located back near Tranmere. His watch was found to have stopped at four twenty-seven. Both men were later conveyed to the Watson Street mortuary where their bodies were formally identified by their fathers. An inquest held at the Victoria Hotel, Cleveland Street brought in the verdict of found drowned. The foreman of the jury commented on their brave acts of heroism which no doubt reflected their qualities as once excellent yachters and fine young men.

A HAZARDOUS OCCUPATION

On Thursday 27 February 1913, thirty-year-old John Roberts towered high above the people of Birkenhead. He was a window cleaner employed by the Cheshire Window Cleaning Company based in Borough Road and that afternoon was engaged in washing the panes at 25 Slatey Road. At about one-thirty, Mr Roberts somehow lost his balance, and fell from his ladder some 20ft to the ground. In his rapid descent he knocked against his colleague, Percy Garrett, who was working on windows below him. Luckily he was unhurt, but John crashed down to the concrete pavement below. Garrett peered over and saw John lying groaning in agony. An ambulance was sent for and Percy escorted John to the Borough Hospital. On the way he complained pitifully of the colossal pain he was suffering in his neck. On admittance Dr West, senior house surgeon, found the patient to be suffering from shock and concussion. There was an extensive wound to the left side of his head and it was bleeding profusely. His only hope was an immediate operation, and Dr Mill was sent for to perform it. Sadly the procedure resulted in haemorrhaging and it was realised that the unlucky cleaner's chances of recovery were almost non-existent. He died at twelve-fifteen the following morning. An inquest regarding the death was held on Saturday 1 March before the borough coroner. Death was due to haemorrhage as a result of fracture to the skull.

A map from 1912 depicting Slatey Road, Oxton.

AN IMPRUDENT YOUTH

Late in the afternoon of 8 January 1901, James Crawley, of 14 Earl Street, Rock Ferry, was waiting for his workmates to clock off for the day at Messrs Price and Reeves, railway contractors. The youth was employed as a messenger for the company between the Rock Ferry Bridge and Parkfield Bridge. He caught sight of his friend Richard Thomas who had worked with him for about a month. The seventeen-year-old looked after the railway men's tea cans and it was usual for him to walk home with James and a group of other lads each evening. They greeted each other and soon set off for the short cut home. It was their custom to dart across the railway track near Rock Lane West, as this was the quickest, albeit not the safest way home.

Richard made his way over the fence separating the new works being laid from the main line. He gained a footing and slowly scaled the railings. Once over, he stepped

The fatal area of railtrack from a map dated 1899.

back to allow his friend room to follow, waiting in between the metals. Young Crawley secured a grip and started to climb over, ignoring signs placed about the track by the managers warning workmen to stay clear.

Suddenly he was pulled back to the ground by an abrupt tug of his coat. Francis Brown, a driver at the construction works, had warned them several times not to cross the line and knew that at any moment an express was due. He admonishingly shouted over to Richard hoping to get his attention, but it was too late. His sight was caught by the billowing black smoke emanating furiously from the funnel of a rapidly approaching locomotive.

'Richard!' James cried.

Richard desperately tried to get clear of the track, but sadly he was not quick enough. Mr Brown, Crawly and the other boys watched in horror as the 5.05 from Chester struck the lad. The speeding engine's left buffer shattered his leg before launching the teenager onto the stone trackside. The train then continued down the line; its driver would know nothing of the accident until he had reached Woodside.

Dr Temple was called for and soon arrived with his equipment. However it immediately became apparent that there would be no need for it. Richard's skull had been fractured to an incredibly severe extent. His right leg was broken and there was a catalogue of other terrible injuries. There was no doubt in the doctor's mind that death would have been instantaneous.

PC Garrett was contacted, and he made arrangements for the deceased to be taken to a mortuary. It was there that Richard's mother, Mary, tearfully identified the body as that of her son.

On the afternoon of Thursday 10 January an inquest was held into the circumstances surrounding the regrettable railway fatality and a verdict of accidental death was returned.

GUILLOTINED

On the afternoon of Thursday 5 January 1899 a most dreadful accident occurred at the hydraulic accumulator on the south side of the West Float. William Ramsey, a twenty-four-year-old labourer who resided at 31 Hope Street, was carrying out his usual work when James Calderbank, a joiner and fellow employee of the Mersey Dock and Harbour Board, shouted over to Ramsey asking if he could fetch him some tools. The labourer obliged and made his way up to the railed platform to acquire the joinery equipment. He located them at once and on peering over saw that James was patiently waiting on ground level. William then went to the railings to lower the tools. Tragically, he failed to keep clear of the dangerous hydraulic machinery that had suddenly been put into motion. The descending accumulator plunged down in an instant, firmly compressing Williams' neck between the railings and practically tearing it in half. Shocked workers who witnessed the unexpected beheading of one of their workmates looked on aghast as blood oozed from the wound. The body slumped back and slowly the crimson liquid began pumping from the platform onto the horror-struck workers below. 'Something has burst', called out a labourer.

'No Jimmie, it's blood!'

PC Wright arrived at the float and had Williams conveyed to the Borough Hospital by a horse ambulance. Doctor Hare immediately pronounced his patient dead, remarking that the unfortunate man had probably died in an instant.

In future the staff at the West Float no doubt took greater care when operating what was potentially lethal and most destructive machinery.

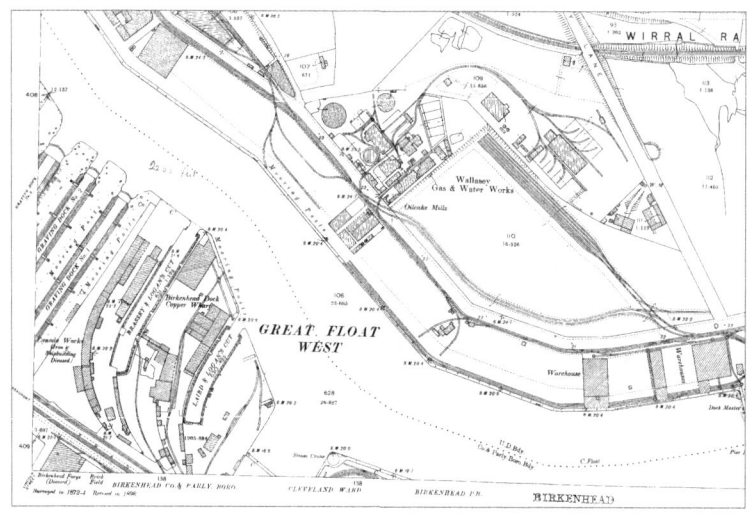

The West Float from a map dated 1899.

A HARMFUL HESITATION

On Monday 3 February 1913, teacher Annie Gaskill was walking near the grand and imposing entrance to Birkenhead Park in Conway Street. That afternoon she noticed a large group of children playing at the roadside and could hear the childish screams and shouts that she was so used to in her occupation.

On the road she watched as a motor car approached. On seeing the group of cheerful kids the driver slowed the vehicle down to avoid any dreadful mishaps. The driver's foresight was most fortunate, as at that moment a young girl ran into the road, unaware of the vehicle travelling towards her. The driver, Thomas Whittaker Berry, sounded the horn in an irritable manner, and eight-year-old Nellie Linaker suddenly noticed the danger in which she had placed herself. Both the car and the girl came to a complete halt in the middle of the road. Mr Moon, the owner of the car, was quite perplexed at the unscheduled stop and wished his driver would recommence the journey at once.

Whittaker Berry restarted the car, sounded his horn once again and began to judder forward, thinking that the reckless girl was about to run back to the pavement out of harm's way. As the car sped up, Nellie hesitated and failed to move out of the path of the oncoming vehicle. She was hit hard and knocked to the ground.

Conway Street, Birkenhead, as seen on a map from 1911.

The little girl's playmates became distressed at the sight of her limp body, which lay motionless on the ground. Nellie

Above: The park entrance as it would have looked at the time of Nellie Linaker's tragic death.

The same stretch of road as it appears in 2007.

was taken to Borough Hospital and examined by junior house surgeon Dr Allen. He could see no trace of physical injury but the poor girl could not be revived. She died at half-past-seven that evening. Death was due to shock.

THE WIDOW WORRIERS

In July 1901 an appalling tragedy was brought to light at a certain house in Rock Ferry. Up until the January of that year, an elderly widow had resided at the property with only an older sister for companionship. Sadly in that month the latter of the two women died, leaving the younger sibling, seventy-year-old Mary Ockleston, living alone.

Not long afterwards a fellow widow came to the address at 144 Bedford Road and took up a room as a paying guest. Mrs Emily Stonehouse was a highly educated woman with a number of successful relatives in both Rock Ferry and Liverpool. The two ladies were the only occupants of the house, but occasionally Mrs Ockleston employed a neighbouring woman to carry out some light domestic work.

The pair of friendly widows were well known in the area and could often be seen strolling about the town together. On Friday 12 July the helpful charwoman

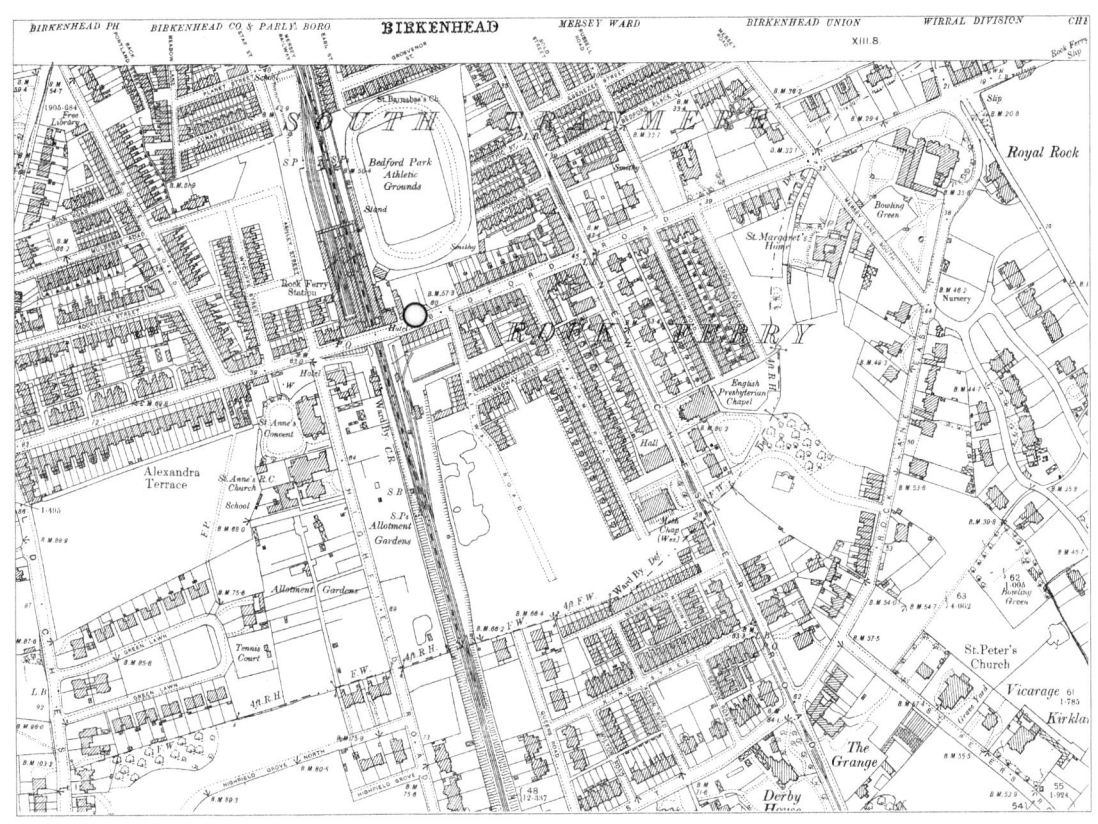

Bedford Road, Rock Ferry, from a map dated 1899.

realised that the usually inseparable companions had not been seen for about two days. She made some general enquires among the local townspeople and learned that Mrs Ockleston had been seen making purchases at a number of shops on Wednesday evening, whereas Mrs Stonehouse had not been seen for some time previously, and that neither of the widows had been spotted since. Concerned, the caring charwoman returned to her cottage behind the house on Bedford Road and informed her husband of her worries.

On the Saturday morning her spouse made his way round to the house to check whether the elderly residents were alright and to put his wife's fretful mind at ease. A succession of knocks on the front door yielded no response and, after waiting for some time, he secured a ladder and placed it firm against an open bedroom window at the rear of the building. He scrambled carefully up the ladder and through into the house, finding himself in a bedroom. The good-intentioned intruder called out for the two ladies. 'Mrs Ockleston? Mrs Stonehouse?' But there was no response.

He anxiously made his way through the upper floor before stumbling across a dreadful scene. The septuagenarian Mrs Ockleston was lying on the floor in a most helpless and dazed condition. She seemed to be suffering from some sort of mental imbalance and was behaving most unlike her usual self. In the next bedroom, the charwoman's husband could see Mrs Stonehouse. She was lying fully clothed, outstretched on a bed. He went over to see if she was alright, but it soon became clear that the middle-aged tenant was dead. With Mrs Ockleston rolling about incoherently on the floorboards, the man hurriedly descended the stairs and ran out to fetch help.

A view down Bedford Road in about 1910.

Bedford Road, Rock Ferry, 2007.

The police soon arrived on the scene, as did Dr Newington, who was known to be the two ladies' medical attendant. On examination the doctor declared that Mrs Stonehouse had been dead for what was in his opinion three days at the least. With regard to Mrs Ockleston, Dr Newington surmised that owing to the way she had been living, taking little or nothing to eat, her fragile mind had become too weak to notice or even realise the death of her companion on the bed, let alone act in her once respectable manner.

It was arranged for a horse ambulance to take Mrs Ockleston to the Borough Hospital for treatment. Medical staff administered the unintelligible woman with several restoratives and by the following Sunday she had begun to show a vast improvement and was progressing favourably.

The facts of the case were later related to the borough coroner Mr Cecil Holden, but as Dr Newington had been attending the deceased for some time, he was prepared to issue a death certificate stating alcoholism as the cause of death. The registrar was prepared to accept such a conclusion and an inquest was found not to be necessary. The certificate was issued and a Liverpool firm of undertakers subsequently removed the body for interment.

THE BEBINGTON SHOWGROUND DISASTER

The opening days of 1916 were turbulent as the worst storm the borough had experienced for a decade battered the area relentlessly. The year was literally blown in as gales swept hard across Wirral causing the utmost damage and distress. There were many reports of elderly people being lifted from the ground in their endeavours to get about the streets, battling the miserably wet weather. Neither was it an uncommon occurrence for pedestrians to be hurled to the ground, and numerous cases of superficial injuries were treated by local doctors. In the north end of Birkenhead, one young man suffered a rather nasty head injury from a falling coping stone. In Tranmere, the roof of the football stadium was ripped up and

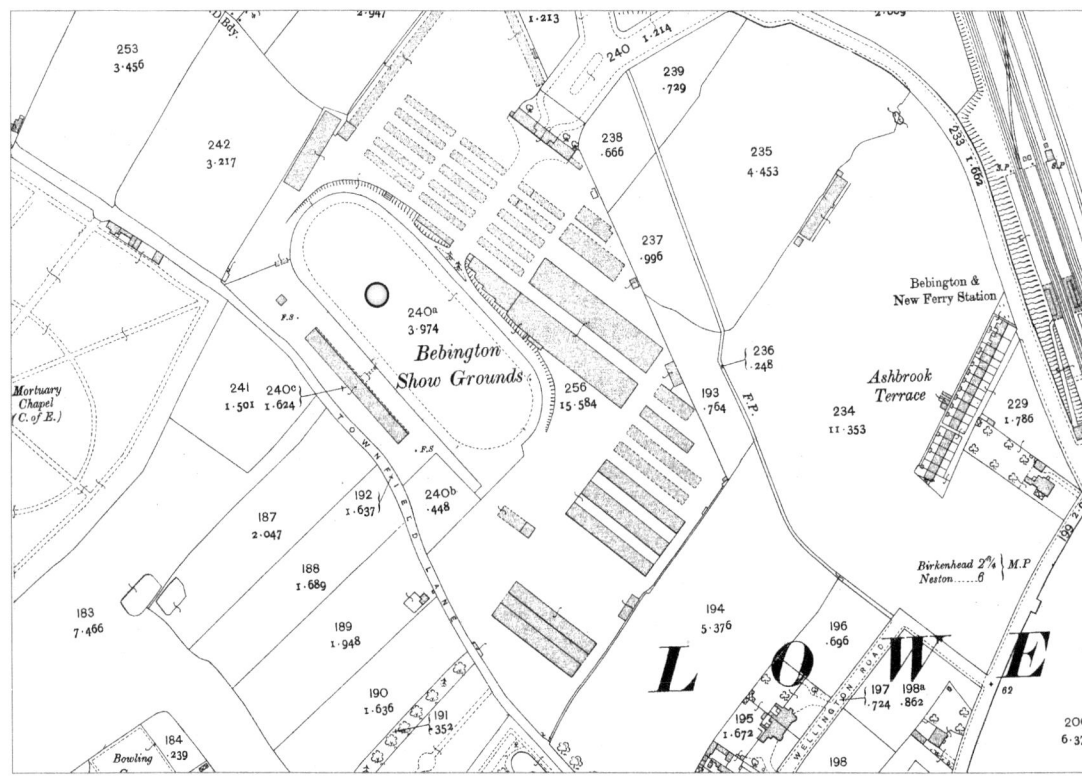

The Bebington Showgrounds, now The Oval, as seen on a map from 1912.

The aftermath of the destructive gale which struck Bebington in January 1916.

carried high across the road before landing in a field opposite. Later the eastern stand to which it had been attached was itself levelled, bringing much startled attention from neighbouring residents. Elsewhere in Elmswood Road, a hoarding was flattened, and at Central station a brick wall disintegrated onto the pavement. In Downham Road a pane of newly fixed plate glass was torn clean from its framework and smashed to smithereens. Fortunately the shop it adorned was unoccupied at the time. In Whetstone Lane the window of a sweet shop opposite the fire station was blown in, and in Oxton, a chimney was wrenched from its fixings. Bricks and plaster were hurled into the grate causing considerable unease to the people inside. A great commotion took place as their house rapidly began to fill with black smoke.

A huge tree in Highfield, Rock Ferry, fell across the cinder path walk leading to Bebington; the branches and leaves creating a rather pretty archway under which walkers were forced to pass. In Lower Bebington several houses in the course of their construction were blown in, much to the dismay of building staff.

By far the most disastrous result of the storm was witnessed at the Bebington Showgrounds, now known as the Oval.

On Saturday 1 January approximately sixty soldiers belonging to C Company were garrisoned inside a large shed-like building. Before the military began to occupy the space in October it was used to house horses. Now the stable boxes had been removed and the interior totally refurbished. It measured 85yds in length and was

90ft wide. The two brick walls were surmounted by a corrugated iron roof held together in sections by iron stays.

That afternoon many of the men billeted there were taking an afternoon nap, but a few were sitting up and a small group of others were playing cards in the centre of the room. Private Dyer was lying down, but he could not sleep because of the howling wind swirling about outside. He noticed the building start to sway. This was not unusual as it had been doing so intermittently for most of the afternoon. Neither he nor any of the other soldiers took any notice of the property's foreboding movement. Then came a second, harder gust and a low rumbling could be heard above the wind. Some soldiers looked up and it was then that they noticed the roof start to lift. Moments later the solid iron stays began to buckle.

'Run boys, it's falling in!' Dyer shouted as he fled from his bed to the nearest exit.

A painful squeak of bolts was heard and the outer wall burst forward, crashing onto the soldiers attempting to escape. Seconds later the north end gable fell forward before the 60-ton iron roof it was supporting broke apart; a number of its sections were carried off into the sky like metallic parachutes. The wind, rain and bricks poured in from all sides trapping a number of men beneath the rubble.

The entrance to the Oval, 2007.

The funeral procession of Private Tinsley.

Those who escaped raised the alarm and soon about 400 fellow recruits were on hand to dig out the rubble and save those trapped beneath it. Colonel Ashby and Captain and Adjutant Beardwood directed the rescue operation. The Birkenhead Fire Brigade, Ambulance Service and workers of the Voluntary Aid Detachment soon began offering their services. In addition several taxi drivers in the vicinity kindly conveyed those injured to the Borough Hospital. One of these victims was Private Connor. He was bleeding profusely from injuries received when a portion of the roof struck his head and legs. He was dragged from the devastation by a number of willing hands after an entrance was cut to free him. Elsewhere others were found sitting in an upright position. They had not been as fortunate as those who had managed to escape from their beds in time and had suffered substantial cuts and bruises.

Under a heap of bricks and part of the roof were discovered a pair of protruding feet. Upon removal from the masonry the man's injuries proved to be so severe that at that time he could not be identified by his comrades. Miraculously he was not dead, only unconscious. He was carefully placed into an ambulance and sent for medical treatment in Birkenhead, however, the injuries he received during the accident were so dire that he died on the way to hospital.

Dr Bentley received the body shortly after death. He noted that the deceased had suffered a fractured skull. His face was flattened and the left side of his head was depressed. This was evidence that the dead man had been lying on his back at the time the building fell on top of him.

It transpired that this victim, the one and only fatality of the disaster, was Private William Tinsley of Wigan, who was attached to the second Cheshires Garrison Battalion. The twenty-nine-year-old was residing at 29 King Street, Bolton, and was married with two children.

Those injured and suffering from shock included: Lance-Corporal Beal, Corporal Croft, Privates Pickford, Doolan, Entwistle, Lally, Ashcroft, O'Gara, Connor and Houghton. Beal was suffering from a broken leg and injuries to the back. Ashcroft had received severe injuries to the head, back and legs.

An inquest was held by the deputy coroner Mr Cotton on the following Tuesday. Mr Cotton had spoken to Professor Plummer of Bidston Observatory, who had reliably informed him that the storm on Saturday was the worst the Wirral had seen for ten years. There was no doubt that the building collapsed as a result of this tremendous and abnormal wind pressure.

Captain Beardwood and coroner's officer Moore described how they had had great difficulty in tracking down the whereabouts of Mr Tinsley's widow. It was believed that she was now living in Liverpool and every effort was being made to inform her of the sad death of her husband. A verdict of accidental death was returned.

A DEDICATED VILLAGE

In the spring of 1909, great anxiety was felt in Port Sunlight as rumours spread that the small purpose-built village was ablaze. Shortly after nine o'clock on the morning of Wednesday 21 April residents could see huge plumes of thick black smoke coming from the area which appeared to confirm the unwelcome news. There was a great rush of people towards the village, all anxious as to its ominous-looking fate. On arrival people soon found that the destruction was not as bad as they had first imagined. Indeed, there was a fire, but it had been quickly attended to almost as soon as it had first ignited.

It was discovered that the outbreak had occurred among several large barrels of resin. These containers were stored at the rear of the printing works on an open plot of land which was surrounded by the rail track from Spital junction. At the time of the incident several wagons loaded with slack were stored on this area. Near to these vehicles lay a large quantity of fuel which served as a sort of embankment.

Owing to some unknown cause, the barrels of resin, a highly flammable substance, burst into flames. Their contents were soon burning fiercely and spread among the whole stockpile of barrels. On discovery of the fire the alarm was raised and a mass of workmen ran from the factory and began to quell the flames with the aid of hoses. Quick-thinking staff proceeded to dig a trench around the inferno to prevent the flames from taking hold of a second pile of barrels only a short distance away.

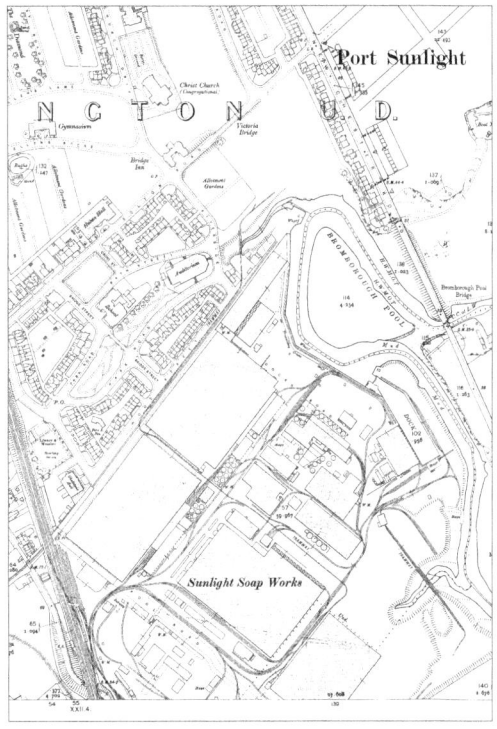

Port Sunlight on a map dated 1912.

The Port Sunlight Fire Brigade, under the direction of Superintendent Famery, was swiftly on the scene, followed closely by the Birkenhead Fire Brigade. He and Superintendent Burns both got to work in a most energetic manner. A steamer was ordered to be put into action and at once began pumping water from the nearby hydrants. The dense smoke, together with the searing heat proved to be extremely difficult to contend with; no sooner had one blazing barrel been extinguished than a

A multi-view postcard of Port Sunlight in 1916.

second, third and fourth began to heat up again. The sides of two coal trucks were badly burned and it was clear that the damage done would have been considerably worse if it wasn't for the prompt action of the firefighters.

Superintendent Burns suffered scalding from some of the resin overflowing into his boots, but he refused to let such a minor mishap detain him from his duty. Several other men also received injuries, but fortunately they did not prove to be serious.

By one o'clock, the fire was completely extinguished. It was later estimated that a total of 1,000 barrels were destroyed at a cost of about £4,000.

The way in which Messrs Lever's employees reacted was a magnificent testament to their loyalty to the firm. Labourers or clerks, one and all without distinction had courageously faced the flames in a combined effort to cut short their progress. Undoubtedly, had it not been for the swift action of these men the fire would have spread to Lord Lever's celebrated soap works, an occurrence which could have had most disastrous consequences.

A BRAVE MAYOR

On the evening of 21 November 1912, the Mayor, J.T. Thompson and his wife were scheduled to attend the Church Choir Festival which was being held in Liverpool's famous St George's Hall. The civic couple donned their coats and hats, made their way out of their home in Chetwynd Road, Oxton, and climbed into an awaiting carriage. The alderman told his driver that they wished to travel to Hamilton Square in order to catch a train to Lancashire. The driver proceeded to take hold of the reins and started the horses on the short journey to the station.

Upon reaching the junction of Cearns Road and Alton Road the cab smashed into a second vehicle, a taxi cab, and the resulting damage was exceedingly severe. The windows of the taxi were shattered sending shards of broken glass all over the leafy suburban street. The shaft of the carriage was broken, the foot-board knocked to bits and the back axle totally destroyed. The horses leapt about in their terror and dragged the carriage up onto the pavement, snapping their traces in the process. Pedestrians ran from the footpath out of harm's way as the mayor and mayoress were hurled about inside the carriage. Once the vehicles were stable, locals who witnessed the incident came to assist the mayor and take charge of the horses.

On being assisted out of the carriage, the occupants were naturally quite shaken by their experience. Nevertheless, the mayor brushed himself down and insisted that he and his wife would continue on to Liverpool in a taxi of their own. This they duly hailed and they sped off down the road.

Unfortunately the occupants of the cab which had collided head-on with the mayor's carriage were not so lucky. Miss Allen, her brother and their elderly mother, all from Mount Pleasant, sustained some rather nasty cuts in the incident and were naturally somewhat distressed at what had just occurred.

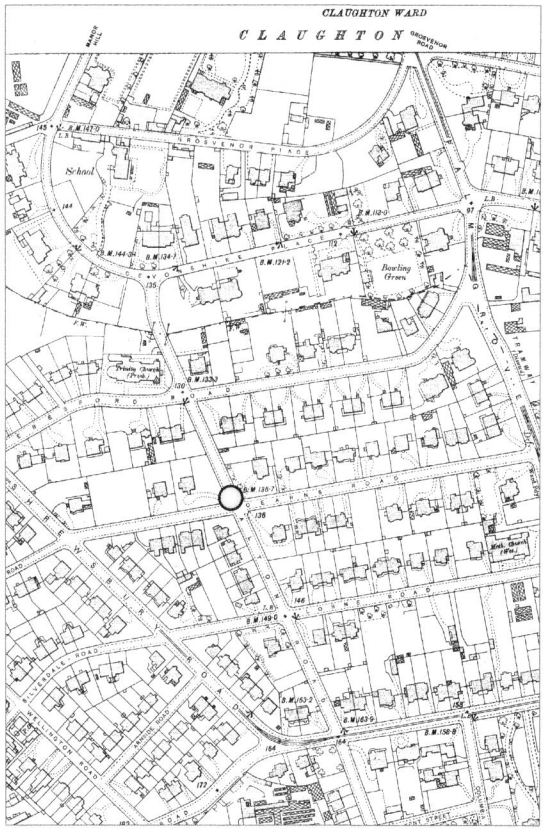

The junction of Cearns Road and Alton Road on a 1912 map.

The junction of Cearns Road and Alton Road, 2007.

Happily, Alderman Thompson and his consort were uninjured. They were observed to be most calm and relaxed throughout the evening's vocal performance. None of their friends who spoke to them that evening could have possibly imagined the peril they had just endured.

A DEVOTED BROTHER

On the sunny afternoon of Wednesday 10 June 1908 four-year-old Henry Wilson was playing with his younger sister Esther in Victoria Park, Tranmere. The two children were running about gleefully, enjoying the fresh air and sunshine which their scenic surroundings provided in abundance. Yet this happy scene was soon to change. The doting siblings made their way across to Albany Road at the far side of the park. Fenced in the field there stood a gloomy clay pit pool. It was 5ft deep and the water rather murky. Continuing their fun, three-year-old Esther decided to climb through the barrier and scrambled aboard a large plank of wood which was floating attractively in the water just like a toy raft. To her horror it immediately overturned, plunging her into the cloudy depths of the pit. Her brother Henry, himself only small, waded into the water in a desperate attempt

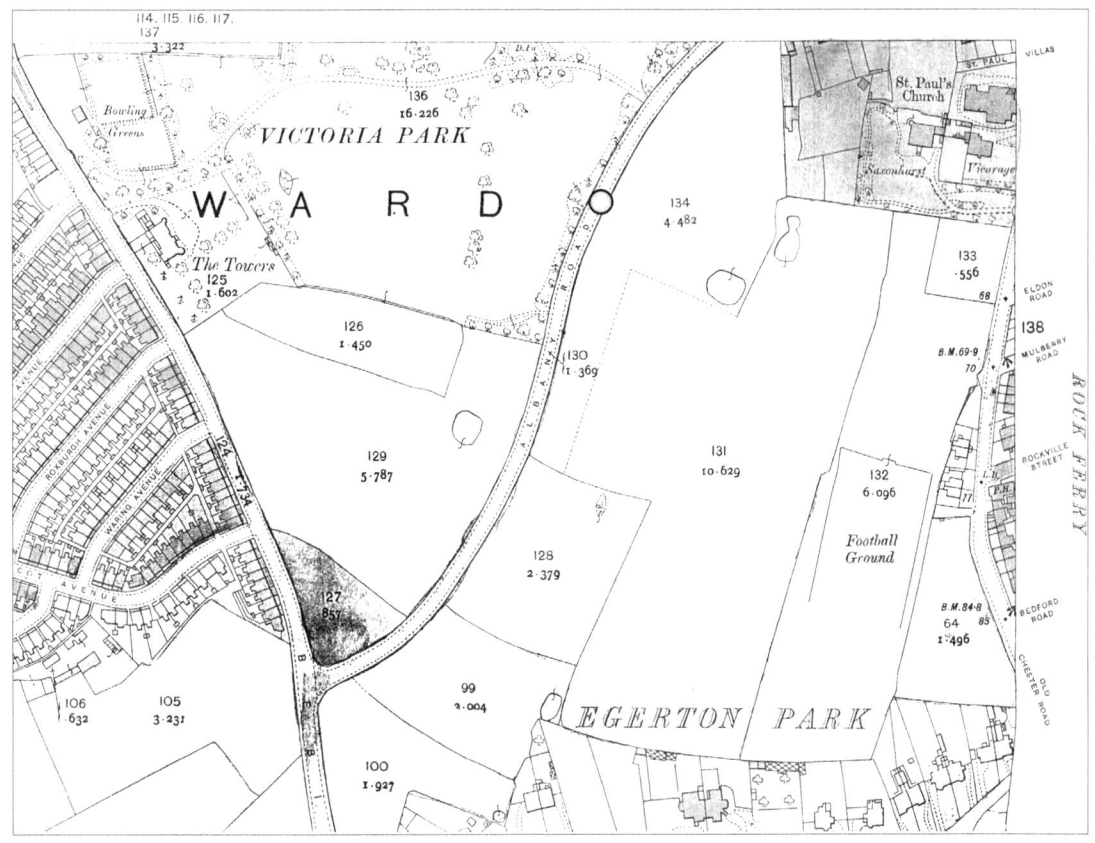

The vicinity of Victoria Park and Albany Road on a 1912 map.

to save his drowning sister. He got in as far as his neck and reached out in a panic-stricken bid to rescue Esther. He stretched his arm out as much as he could, but she was too far away. Henry climbed aboard the wooden plank and heaved himself to the grass shore. With his clothes dripping wet, he cried his way back into the park screaming for help.

A number of people who had been lounging at leisure on the grass came to his assistance and ran over to the clay pit. Archibald Cullen of 27 Meadow Lane, and Charles Witham of 10 Wye Street, wasted no time in stripping down to their underclothes and jumping in to search for the lost child. The water was so opaque it seemed that the girl would never be found unless the pit was drained. However, Mr Cullen successfully managed to locate the girl by feeling about with his feet. She was lying face upwards about three or four yards from the edge on the pool. He ducked under the water and lifted her out.

PC Griffiths was beckoned as he neared the scene and upon seeing the body instantly began an attempt at resuscitation. Unfortunately this was to no avail.

A horse ambulance was telephoned and Esther was conveyed to the Wirral Children's Hospital in Woodchurch Road. There Dr Berry, the resident medical officer, pronounced life to be extinct. An inquest was held on the following Thursday before the Borough Coroner who announced:

'The action of the little boy was extremely remarkable and was a wonderful exhibition of courage and presence of mind. It was unfortunate that his efforts to save his little sister were unsuccessful. The conduct of the two men was also

An early twentieth-century view of Victoria Park, Tranmere.

Albany Road, Tranmere, with Victoria Park on the left, 2007.

excellent. They acted with great promptitude in what must have been very trying circumstances and they deserve the greatest credit'.

Speaking through their foreman, the jury endorsed Mr Holden's remarks and also expressed their most sincere sympathy to Mr Moses Wilson and his wife. They had lost their only daughter and the distressing incident had had a painful impact upon their neighbours in the Town Road area. The jury returned a verdict of accidentally drowned.

RIFLE RESPITE

On Monday 4 April 1904 the steamer *Richmond* was making a return trip on the Mersey from the city of Chester. Aboard were members of the 1st Cadet Battalion Liverpool Regiment. Other members of the regiment had decamped and were marching out to meet the steamer and accompany the vessel on its return journey. The boat conveying the cadets had not long left Eastham ferry stage when a shot was suddenly heard and all eyes turned in the direction of the ear-piercing sound. Sergeant Benjamin Williams fell to the deck; it was obvious that he was injured and in considerable pain. Assistance was immediately rendered by Sergeant Edward Bowman and Valentine McLennon, the latter being a member of the London and North Western Ambulance Corps. The pair knelt beside him keen to establish the cause of the man's agonising cries.

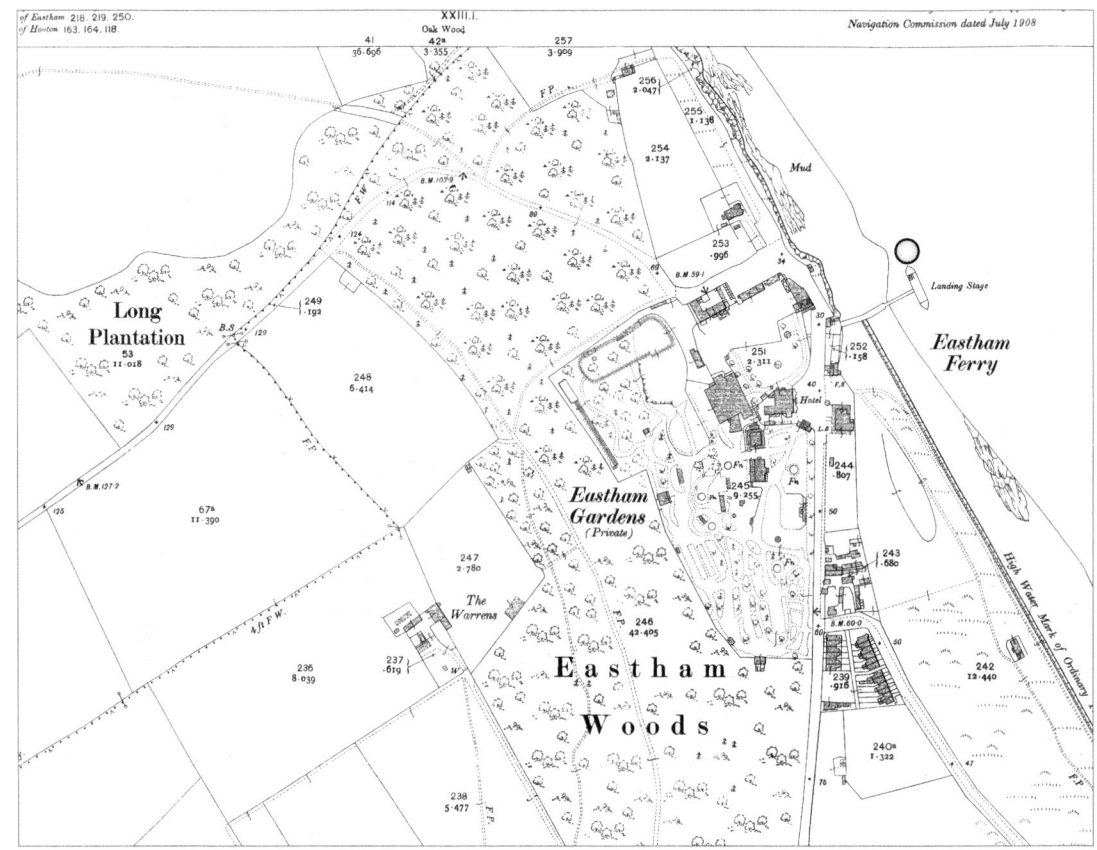

Eastham Ferry on a map dating from 1911.

Eastham Ferry, c. 1905.

A great commotion was witnessed as all those on board hurried round Sergeant Williams to discover the details of the affair. It was quickly seen that the victim of the mysterious mishap was bleeding profusely from his armpit; it seemed he had been shot.

Those on board recalled how just before they watched Sergeant Williams collapse, he had been quite happily resting upright on his rifle. It was concluded that either he or a fellow soldier must have unwittingly come into contact with the trigger and sent a bullet speeding directly through the man's shoulder blade.

It was presumed that the rifle would not have been loaded, but evidently a cartridge must have been forgotten about and left inside the chamber. The result was a most tragic calamity, for the non-commissioned officer's condition soon began to deteriorate.

Before long the boat berthed alongside the landing stage at Liverpool where Major Leslie signalled for an ambulance. The desired help rapidly arrived from the Northern Hospital and Sergeant Williams was conveyed there for treatment. He was immediately attended to and his health began to improve. Doctors found that the bullet that had wounded the volunteer was, fortunately for him, only a blank.

Subsequent inquiries by the Battalion into Sergeant Williams' condition revealed that he was progressing favourably and was as well as could be expected under the circumstances.

A DEEP SLEEP

On the morning of 30 October 1913, Dr Noble rushed anxiously up the stairs of 23 Cavendish Drive, Bebington. Upon entering a bedroom he found thirty-seven-year-old Bertram Langley lying unconscious among the sheets.

'Mr Langley?' the doctor queried, eager to get a reply.

There was no response. The chartered accountant was breathing fairly evenly but could not be roused from his comatose condition. On closer examination Dr Noble found his patient to be perspiring profusely. His skin, which was somewhat discoloured, was covered in sweat.

'Is your husband in the habit of taking a narcotic?' the doctor asked Mrs Langley who was standing behind the doctor praying that he could help her dear spouse. She replied that he sometimes took veronal; a barbiturate used as a hypnotic aid to help him sleep.

Dr Noble told Mrs Langley that she should keep an eye on her husband and that he would call back to the house to examine him again the following day.

The next morning, Halloween, Dr Noble called at the property for a second time, ascended the stairs and made his way into the Langley's bedroom. On this occasion he discovered that Bertram's pulse had greatly increased. On examining his patient's chest the doctor found it to be congested and observed that the man's lips and nails had turned a disturbing shade of blue. There was nothing that could be done except hope that his health improved of its own accord.

On the Saturday morning the doctor again returned to see if Mr Langley had indeed made any sign of improvement. Alas things had become much worse. Bertram had become weaker; his pulse was feeble and his breathing was now very laboured. Dr Noble was now quite pessimistic regarding any chance of recovery and his opinion soon proved to be correct. Bertram Langley died later that day.

Cavendish Drive on a map from 1912.

The Langley residence in Cavendish Drive, as it looked in 2007.

An inquest held at the Coroner's Court by Mr A.F. Cotton inquired into the accountant's death. Doctor Noble stated that a subsequent post-mortem on his patient revealed death was due to syncope consequential of an overdose of veronal and subsequent pneumonia.

'Veronal is a drug about which little is known up to the present?' the Deputy Coroner asked.

'A good deal is known', replied the doctor, 'because it has been used very largely by the public for some time. It did not come under the Poisons Act until last year. Veronal was supposed at one time to be harmless, but it was by no means harmless; in fact it was a very risky thing to take, as in fact most drugs were.'

Mr Chevalier, a Liverpool solicitor who had been a friend of the deceased's for a good many years, stated that the Langleys had always been a very affectionate and loving couple. He produced a statement from Mrs Langley who was still too overcome with grief to appear in court. In it she said that about three months previously her husband confessed to her that he had experimented with a drug. She had written that she had at once admonished him for his foolish actions and since that incident Mrs Langley had not seen her husband take veronal or any other drug of any kind. The deceased was rarely depressed and had never threatened to take his life. As far as Mrs Langley knew they were in no financial difficulty, and even if they were, she had savings of a private means with which she could have helped. Death was due to veronal poisoning inadvertently administered.

SIBLING ADVERSITY

On the afternoon of 29 December 1864, twenty-six-year-old Abel Johnson drove his cart through the sleepy suburbs of Oxton. That day Abel halted his horse at the house of his brother Charles, on the corner of Fairclough Lane. At about twenty minutes past five, Abel stepped down from his cart and made his way up the charming garden path.

In the greenhouse stood Joseph Plevin. He worked as a gardener for the elder Johnson and was tending to some flowers alongside his employer. As Abel entered the greenhouse, Charles's face registered a look of utter infuriation. The two brothers were not the best of friends and even though they were both adults there still lingered an air of bitter sibling rivalry.

'Am I to go to supper with you on Monday?' Abel enquired, hoping to join a family meal being held early next week.

Charles sighed and in no uncertain terms answered that Abel was not to come and scowled as he declared that his brother had only come to his house today to annoy him, as usual. As Abel stood shocked at his brother's blatant rudeness, Charles barged past him and headed out of the greenhouse with much irritation.

Abel attempted to remonstrate with his brother but before he knew what was happening, Charles had got him by the coat and was dragging him down the garden path. He left Abel sitting shaken on the paving.

Charles's labourer had also left the greenhouse and came over to Abel as he sat on the ground like a reprimanded child. Abel suddenly rose and grabbed the gardener by his waistcoat.

An 1875 map showing Fairclough Lane.

'Joseph!' Charles shouted, ordering him to let his foolish brother be. Mr Plevin could smell alcohol on Abel's breath but at that time he was not too noticeably drunk. Charles returned and a second furious struggle commenced between the siblings.

'Charles, do not hurt me', Abel pleaded.

'I do not want to hurt you', Charles gruffly replied, 'I only want to get you away!'

With a firm tug of his collar, the householder managed to forcibly remove the other down to the gate whereupon they both tumbled through it in an almighty heap.

'Just get into the cart', Charles begged as he brushed himself down. He was growing more and more tired of his brother's immature behaviour and wished he would just go back home to South Bank.

'I need my cap'.

Charles sighed heavily before turning back into the garden to fetch the missing hat. On his return Abel began to scuffle once again. It was clear now that he was rather intoxicated.

'You pulled my hair!', yelled Abel.

During the senseless struggle Abel caught his foot on lamp-post, lost his balance and fell backwards onto the pavement. Luckily, Charles managed to grab hold of him and partly break his fall, but this support failed to prevent Abel from banging his head hard against the kerb stone.

Charles fell to his brother's side and for a few moments the younger Johnson seemed dazed and confused.

Charles realised the seriousness of the situation and helped Abel to his feet. He was clutching his head and with the assistance of his brother, Mr Plevin and a local builder by the name of John Thomas, he clambered into the cart, firmly refusing Charles's brotherly offer to climb in and escort him home.

Abel confidently took hold of the reins and trotted off down the road at a brisk pace. On getting to the corner however, he fell into the cart and was suddenly

Fairclough Lane, the quiet and secluded road where the fatal fall occurred.

overcome with dizziness. Mr Plevin came to his aid and drove Mr Johnson back home to his father's house. Samuel Johnson owned a large house in South Bank and also ran a thriving nursery where Abel was employed. On arrival the young man began to feel rather ill and complained of a dreadfully painful headache. Joseph supported Abel into the house before laying him down to rest on a sofa. Mr Plevin then left Abel in the care of his wife, Harriet.

'Harriet, will you bathe my head?' Abel pleaded, as the immense pain continued to pulsate through his skull. His doting wife went off to fetch some hot water. On her return she found her husband had dozed off, so she decided it would be best not to disturb his afternoon slumber. Later, Harriet realised to her horror that Abel had slipped into unconscious and went to seek urgent medical help.

Mr Godden, surgeon, was called to the property at half-past nine and conducted a swift examination. He found Mr Johnson lying quite insensible and upon examining his head, the surgeon found a distinctive bruise about an inch above the right ear. The attendant observed a number of other symptoms suggesting compression of the brain. Mr Godden treated the patient as best as he could and promised to return in the morning. On the Friday the surgeon found the man's health to have declined rapidly and by one o'clock on that afternoon, Abel Johnson had passed away never having regained consciousness.

A post-mortem revealed a large clot of blood, about 2oz in quantity, on the surface of the brain. The right temple bone was fractured and this was likely to have been the cause of death. It was Mr Godden's opinion that a serious fall would have been sufficient to result in such a fatal injury.

An inquest held before Mr Churton at the Queen's Arms Hotel on 24 December enquired into the death. The coroner stated that when the matter was first reported to him he was under the impression that this was to be a case of fratricide, but from hearing the evidence put to him, he hoped that the jury would agree that such a definition was quite unsuitable. After referring to the alleged intemperate habits of the deceased, Mr Churton remarked that it was up to the jury to determine whether Abel Johnson's death resulted from an accidental fall or whether his brother played any part in his demise. If it was proven that any blows were exchanged between the two, then the brother would be put into a responsible and accountable position. However, from the evidence given to him that day it seemed to Mr Churton that Charles Johnson only acted as any other man would have when faced with a drunken nuisance. From witness statements it seemed that the deceased was constantly indulging in drink which led him to become obnoxious not only to his family, but to all those who were unfortunate enough to encounter him in such an intoxicated state. 'When people did give way to habits of this sort then they must now and then expect something unpleasant to occur', remarked Coroner Churton. He further stated that he had received a letter from Major Hornblower of the 1st C.R.V., reporting Charles Johnson to be a fine soldier of very high character. The Major doubted very much that such a respectable man was capable of fratricide. The jury subsequently returned a verdict of accidental death of which the coroner fully concurred.

STARVATION

On the afternoon of Sunday 28 January 1849, Inspector McNeil paid a visit to a, usually empty, house in Oak Street, Birkenhead. He had received information that squatters may have taken over and was keen to remove any such trespassers at once. On entering the dilapidated dwelling he came across a most heart-wrenching scene. Lying dead upon the floor was the body of a woman. At her feet was a baby, also deceased. At a nearby fireplace there huddled together four young children. Their ages ranged from four to ten years and it seemed to the inspector that they were trying to squeeze the last remains of heat from the blackened bars of the grate. The poor creatures sat in front of the corpses of their even colder mother and nine-month-old brother.

The house contained not one piece of furniture nor could one morsel of food be found within the crumbling walls; the surviving children were on the brink of death. The children told the official that they had not tasted anything since Saturday morning, when their mother had distributed a small amount of bread she had somehow obtained.

Mr Downing, a local surgeon, was contacted and he examined the bodies. It was his professional opinion that, as far as an external examination could reveal, both mother and son had perished from starvation.

Later enquiries revealed that the woman was forty-year-old Ellen Kane. She and her children had arrived in Liverpool from Drogheda, Ireland, only a few days previously with only a shilling in her pocket. On crossing the river she took up residence with a relative in Birkenhead until Sunday last, when she and her family stumbled across the property in Oak Street. Ellen forced the door and promptly moved in.

An 1875 map showing Oak Street.

On the previous Wednesday her relative, a woman called Fay, contacted the assistant overseer for a medical relief note on behalf of the Kanes. This was duly received and was taken to the house of Dr Vaughn, the medical officer for the township. Fay however claimed that no notice was taken of the note and consequently Ellen and her baby son James died.

An inquest was held before Henry Churton at the Angel Hotel. When questioned the assistant overseer Mr Harwood denied that any such contact had been made between him and the woman Fay, and upon checking the medical book no record could be found of any such relief note ever being written.

Ann Ellis, Dr Vaughn's servant also denied any such contact. It was she who would usually answer the door to those requesting relief and she could not recall receiving any note from either Fay or Ellen.

Evidence was also heard from the Revd Mr Brown who had been called in to administer spiritual relief on behalf of the parish. He described how upon meeting Ellen he had asked if she had seen a doctor, as to him she seemed rather ill. He claimed that the Irishwoman replied that she did not need one and was fine. Despite his misgivings, the clergyman failed to make any further enquiries.

The whole case seemed to rest upon the woman Fay's evidence, but her word was strenuously denied by the assistant overseer, the deputy reliving officer and the servant to Dr Vaughn.

After thorough deliberation, the jury delivered a verdict of death from starvation. They were of the opinion that the conduct of Mr Harwood, the assistant overseer, Mr McNarney, the relieving officer and Dr Vaughn, were entirely free from blame. They could not however exonerate the assistant reliving officer, Ann Ellis, or the Revd Mr Brown, for had the latter acted with more humane consideration, and the former two with greater care, such a melancholy result may have been avoided.

THE HOYLAKE SPECIAL

On the afternoon of Monday 25 February 1876 sixty-seven-year-old Thomas Beeston and a friend, Samuel Downs, wandered about the small agricultural village of Moreton. The former was a farm bailiff to the Hon. Sir Edward Cust of Leasowe Castle, and had held that position for some time.

The pair enquired about the neighbourhood, calling in on a number of farmers in search of labourers who would be willing to assist the elderly bailiff in ploughing his land. Over the course of the day the pair partook of four glasses of beer; it was thirsty work!

By late afternoon the two headed off to the Plough Inn where they each had a supper of cheese and bread, washed down with some brandy and water. They discussed business with a number of other farmers until sometime between nine and ten o'clock. Once they had finished their meals and concluded the discussions, Thomas and Samuel headed off home. They were joined by another man, a labourer by the name of John Owens, and he and Samuel walked with Mr Beeston through the rather stormy, yet still light evening.

Upon reaching Reed's Lane Thomas said goodbye to his friends and made his own way home through a route near to the railway. He did not seem

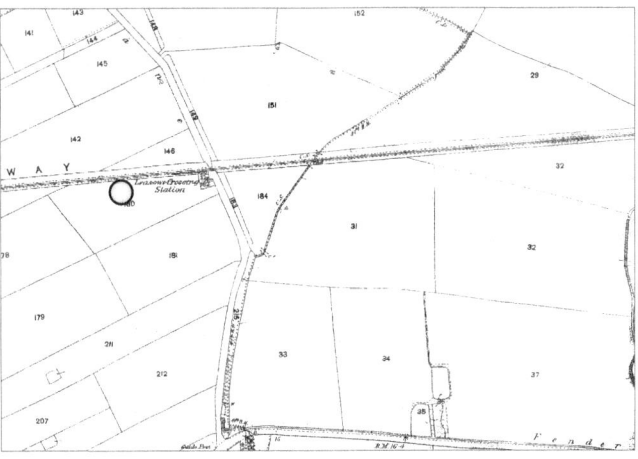

Leasowe Crossing on a map from 1875.

drunk, so Mr Downs and Mr Owens were quite confident in the old bailiff's ability to get to his home safely by himself.

The following morning the body of an elderly man was found on the Hoylake line, near to the Leasowe Crossing. It was Thomas Godwin who discovered the gruesome scene. Early that morning the platelayer found the corpse, which was in a much mangled and mutilated condition. One leg had been completely sliced off, the contorted face was black with bruising and waterlogged brain tissue lay hideously about the track. There was a quantity of blood and hair stuck onto the metals; the trail of death began some 15yds away from the corpse, suggesting that the man had been hit by a train and dragged along for a few seconds before being deposited at the trackside.

The Leasowe Crossing in about 1900, where the body was discovered.

Thomas quickly contacted the authorities and the bloody remains were soon collected up before being taken back to the Plough Inn to await an inquest.

On the following Thursday Mr Churton arrived at the pub to begin his duties as Borough Coroner. David Ridgeway, gateman, deposed that on the night of Monday 25 February, a special train had run from Hoylake to the Docks station and back. Railway manager James Goulding interjected, stating that this was done in order to accommodate a number of passengers who had been delayed in crossing the Mersey to Birkenhead by a previous collision between the locomotives *Cheshire* and *Montana*.

After this interruption Mr Ridgway continued, stating that the special had passed him at the gate at 9.54 and returned at approximately 10.15pm. He was there for some minutes before and said that he had neither seen nor heard anyone on or about the line at that time.

Thomas Humphrey, driver of the special train, recalled that upon passing near to the Leasowe Crossing he had felt something hit the fore part of the engine. He said that he had looked out, but on seeing nothing in the darkness continued on the nocturnal journey. It wasn't until next morning that he found parts of Thomas Beeston's remains on the buffers.

In summing up, the coroner said that according to the evidence the deceased had passed through the gate and wandered down the line instead of crossing it. He appeared to have been sober at that time and his motive for doing so was a total mystery. Mr Churton held the view that Thomas's death was totally accidental and that no blame could be attributed to anyone connected with the railway. The jury subsequently returned a verdict of accidentally killed.

AN EPILEPTIC END

About Christmas 1908 fifty-four-year-old John Hughes took a room in a small terraced house at 51 Rodney Street, Birkenhead. He was an army pensioner but to make ends meet worked as a gateman at the nearby gas works.

On the night of 24 March 1909, Mr Hughes retired to bed in a rather drunken condition. In the early hours of the morning his landlady, Mrs Jones, was awoken by a terrible racket coming from downstairs. She jumped out of bed and wearily went to investigate the cause of the disturbance. Mrs Jones squinted her tired eyes and peered down the darkened staircase. At the bottom she could distinguish the shadowy silhouette of Mr Hughes, and he was making the most unusual sounds. She carefully made her way down to aid her middle-aged tenant whom she discovered had fallen and was now suffering from a severe fit. As he lay shaking on his back, Mrs Jones noticed that John's face was quite bloody with gore slowly dripping from his nose and mouth and a harsh red gash on his wrinkled brow. She noted also that a half-empty whisky bottle lay alongside him.

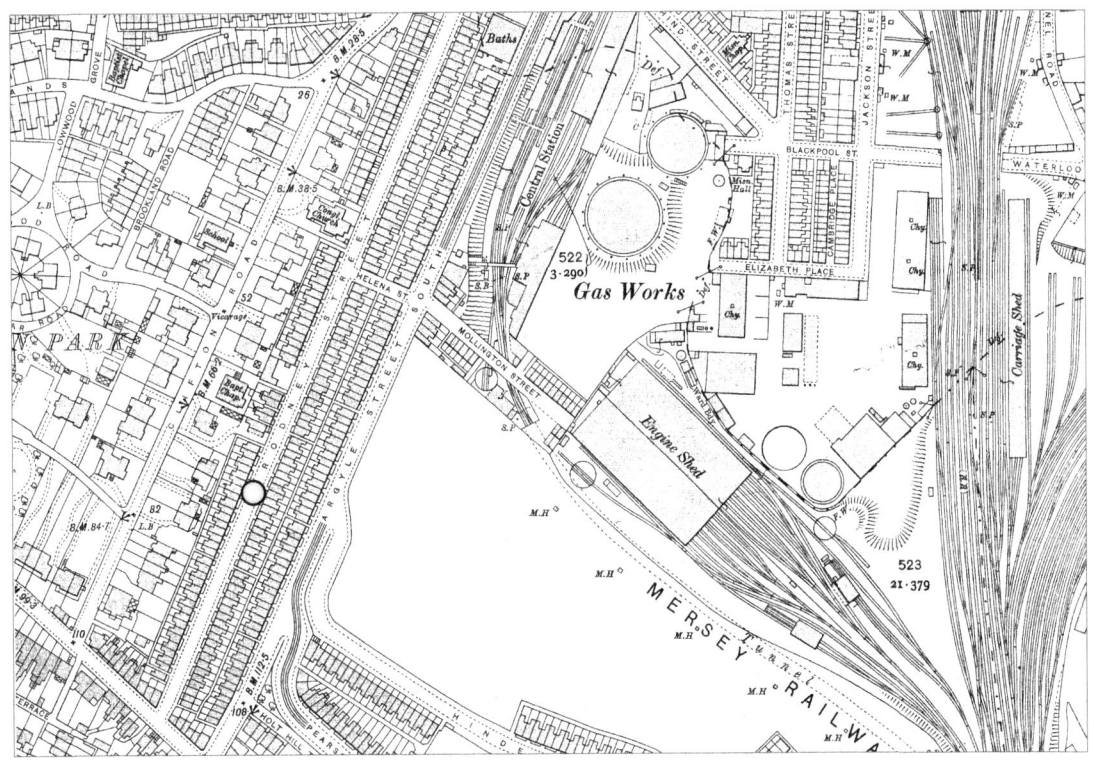

Rodney Street from a map dated 1911.

The house in Rodney Street where John Hughes lived out his final days.

In her nightdress, Mrs Jones managed to help the man to his feet, attended to his wounds and saw him back to bed.

The following day Dr Wilson visited the house and treated Mr Hughes's minor injuries. He had recovered from his earlier distressing seizure and was feeling much better. On the following Sunday morning John had left his lodgings and had gone for a walk along Borough Road. To his dismay he was once again struck down with a fit. He fell to the pavement and began to shake violently at the roadside. A small crowd gathered, including a number of police constables, who upon recognising the epileptic incident came to his aid at once. Mr Hughes's head had become very bruised and grazed and on the pavement was the bloody evidence of the distressing medical condition that had now rendered him unconscious.

The police arranged for the ex-soldier to be taken home and soon his welfare lay in the hands of his landlady, Mrs Jones. His failure to recover from a comatose state gave the woman serious cause for concern. Mrs Jones felt that her lodger needed medical attention, so she contacted the Borough Hospital where a removal order was obtained for treatment. Mr Hughes was examined by Dr Muir, the senior house surgeon, who had his new patient admitted for observation. During that time Mr Hughes suffered several more fits before eventually succumbing on Tuesday evening.

An inquest was held before Cecil Holden on the following Thursday morning. Dr Muir described the cause of death, explaining to the jury that, when first admitted, the deceased was suffering from heavy bruising, particularly about his head. It was his opinion that death was due to epilepsy accelerated by the excessive bruises. The jury returned a verdict in accordance with the medical evidence.

THE LOST BOY

On the evening of Wednesday 5 April 1899 Arthur Rowbottom noticed that his little brother had not returned home from playing. Since the death of their parents, Arthur and his wife Maud had taken on the responsibility of looking after ten-year-old Frank at their home in Brownlow Road, New Ferry. Concerned for the boy's welfare, Mr Rowbottom made enquires and soon learnt that Frank had last been seen playing in a disused claypit at the rear of the house. He made his way round to the pit but could find no sign of his brother. Arthur was becoming anxious, as he had also discovered that Frank had also been playing on a small raft earlier that afternoon which by all accounts was quite unsafe.

Maud told her husband that she had spotted the child in the pit a few hours earlier, but she had warned him to get out and come home or he would drown. The boy did as she asked and came back to Brownlow Road. However, Mrs Rowbottom soon required Frank to go on an errand, and had seen him set out, presuming that he would be back home very shortly. But he had not returned.

Soon the neighbourhood knew of young Rowbottom's disappearance and all were on the lookout. That night seemed like an eternity to Arthur, as he sat waiting for his younger sibling to walk cheerily through the door as he was accustomed to do. Next day and with still no sign of the child, local man John Clarke kindly offered the use of his boat to search the pit, and two young men named Wright earnestly probed about the pond. Their search proved unsuccessful and raised the hope that Frank may not have fallen into the water after all.

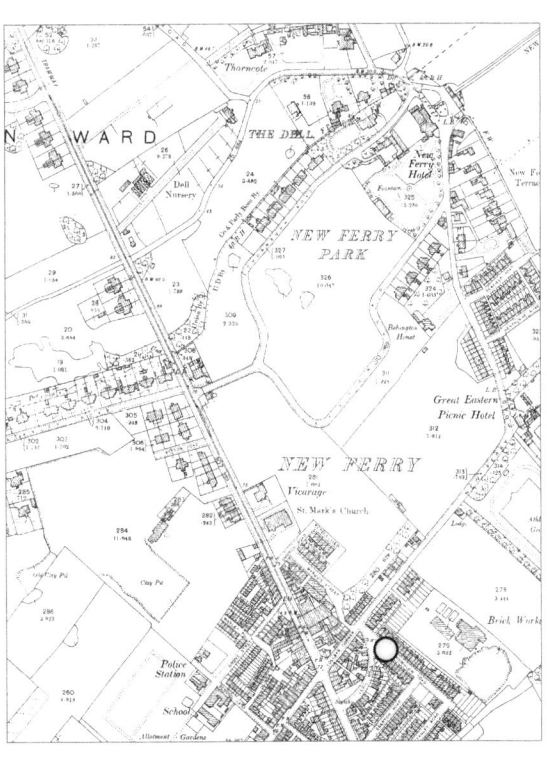

Brownlow Road, New Ferry, as seen on an 1899 map.

On Friday afternoon Sergeant Jackson of the New Ferry police dragged the pit in all directions for quite a substantial amount of time. This too proved fruitless, so in a final attempt the officer fired a charge of blasting powder in the hope of raising anything, or anyone, that may have sunk to the bottom. This idea also failed.

On the Saturday afternoon, Messrs Lever Brothers compassionately sent the Port Sunlight steam fire engine to pump the water. Frederick Bothham set it up and the machine got to work at about six o'clock and continued until four o'clock the following morning. It was then that the body of young Frank Rowbottom was finally discovered. His legs were trapped between two sunken planks; these were held down deep in the water by a sunken truck.

An inquest held at the New Ferry police station by the West Cheshire Coroner allowed the gruesome death to be investigated. Mr J.C. Bate heard how a small boy named John Whitby was one of the last people to see the deceased alive. John deposed that he knew Frank only by sight and had seen him playing on the raft at about noon on Wednesday. The witness was playing on a raft himself, but told Frank he should get to the shore.

'Why?' questioned the coroner, keen to understand the reason behind the boy's apparent hypocrisy.

'It was only a little raft the deceased was on and it was not safe', Whitby replied. Continuing, he stated that he and some other boys left Rowbottom playing at the pit. That was the last they saw of him.

Having briefly addressed the jury, a verdict of accidentally drowned was returned.

A juror suggested that the proprietor of the pit should put up a notice warning that trespassers would be prosecuted. It transpired that there was already such a notice at the entrance so all those who, like Frank Rowbottom, failed to take heed did so at their own peril.

A SHUNTING TRAGEDY

At about ten to seven on the morning of 17 June 1909, thirty-seven-year-old Thomas Weaver kissed his wife goodbye and left his home at 61 Corniche Road, Bebington. He then headed off to his work in the village of Port Sunlight where he was employed as a shunter by Messrs Lever Brothers.

Later that morning Thomas was engaged in the managing of the movement of a number of wagons. He was acting as chief shunter and was supervising George Smith, a fellow employee. Smith had just drawn eight wagons from number one warehouse over to number two warehouse and was now about to start transporting a second set of wagons up the line. On board, Mr Weaver was riding on the footplate.

'Run ahead and stop short', he ordered, as he stepped down from the engine steps. The vehicle was travelling at an unthreatening 4mph when Smith turned his head inside the cab and grasped the regulator. This meant that he could no longer see the line, or his supervisor who had just stepped down to the trackside. Seconds later, Mr Smith noticed that the wagons were slowly rising. He leant out of the cab to see what was causing this unusual motion. To his horror, he saw the legs of a man lying across the line. He at once halted the engine and ran along the footpath towards the lifeless limbs. Thomas Weaver had been run over and now one of the engine's wheels

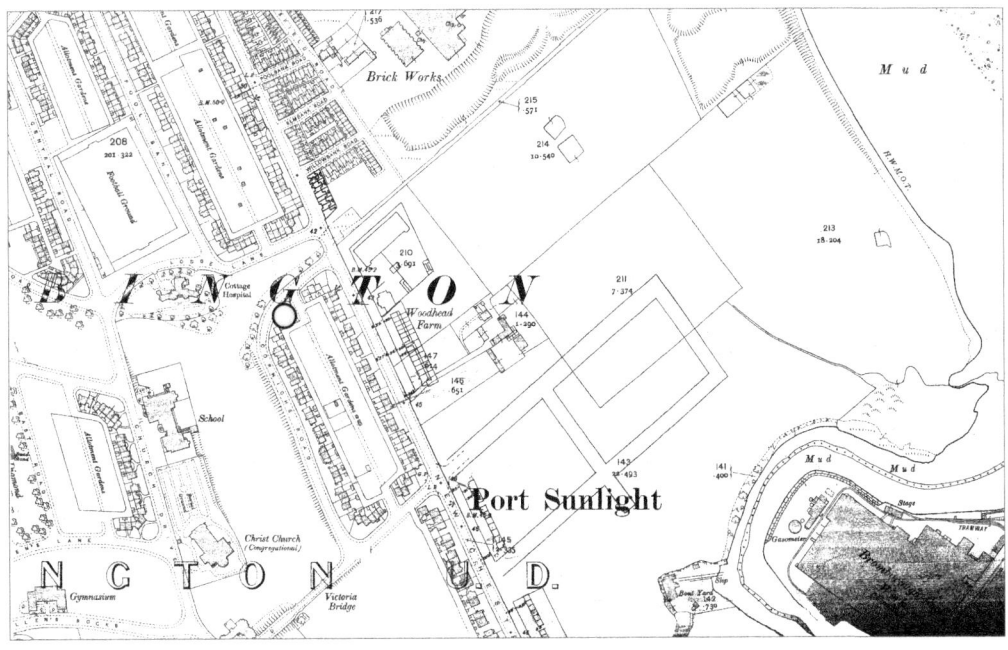

A 1912 map showing Corniche Road, Port Sunlight.

Corniche Drive, Port Sunlight, as it looked in the mid-1910s.

was actually pinning him by the waist. Smith whistled to attract help. George Edward Dickinson, a youth who worked in a stamping room, was taking some wood to a truck when he saw the accident. He had seen how Mr Weaver was struck by a wagon while alighting from another. He was thrown into the path of the engine and four of its wheels passed painfully over his midriff. To Master Dickinson, it seemed that the shock of the tragedy had rendered Weaver senseless, as he did not appear to try and save himself.

Frederick Parkings, another shunter at the works, heard the urgent whistle and ran to the scene. He was onboard the train when the accident occurred and knew something was amiss. He also observed Mr Weaver's body lying on the line.

At about ten o'clock Sergeant Charles Fraser was informed of the accident and he immediately visited the works surgery, where Thomas had been conveyed. Sergeant Fraser had the body taken to the Port Sunlight Cottage Hospital to await an inquest.

On the following Saturday an inquest was held before the West Cheshire Coroner Mr J.C. Bate at New Ferry police station. Mr Bate listened carefully to the witness statements and concluded that shunting operations were about the most dangerous work in connection to the railway. In spite of this, there was no record of any similar accident ever taking place at the works. The distance between the tracks had always been the same, 2ft, and owing to the nature of warehouses this was deemed sufficient. After a brief consultation, the jury returned a verdict of accidental death.

Mr Stubbs, in expressing sympathy on behalf of Messrs Lever Brothers to the Weaver family stated that the deceased bore an excellent character, was a good workman and was well liked by all with whom he came into contact.

A PLUMBER TO THE RESCUE

On Monday 11 May 1908 a young woman by the name of Miss Taylor was carrying out her domestic duties at the home of Mrs Astbury, Park Way, Meols. The maid was busily engaged with some washing in the kitchen when her dress somehow came into contact with the boiler fire. She quickly became a mass of flames, which rapidly engulfed her.

Miss Taylor's bloodcurdling screams attracted the attention of Mr Jones, a local plumber who was working next door. He hurried to the scene where he was aghast to discover the maid running about the yard with her clothing ablaze. With no thought for his own safety, he threw Miss Taylor to the ground and covered her with his coat. Bravely he fought to suppress the flames, but they proved to be too fierce for a mere garment to tackle. The plumber shouted for a nearby boy to go and fetch a rug from the house without delay. This was quickly done and the carpet smothered the flames, although Miss Taylor's dress remained hot and she was crying out in agony. With his bare hands Mr Jones tore the searing clothes from her to prevent any more pain.

Medical help was sought but none could be found, forcing Miss Taylor to be taken by a cab to the Cottage Hospital. En route they came across Dr Thorpe who clambered into the vehicle and aided the stricken servant. Sadly, it was clear to him that

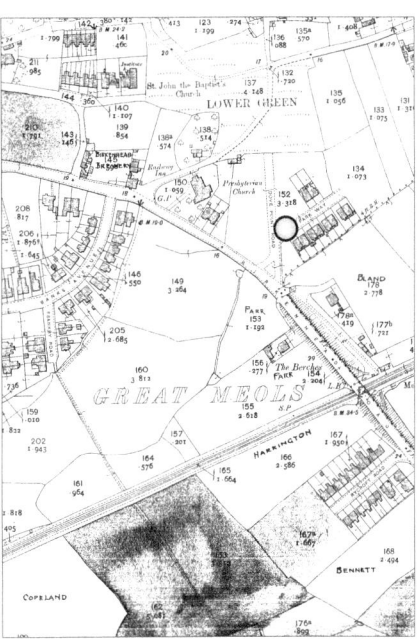

Park Way in Great Meols on a map from 1912.

the woman's injuries were so severe that she would be lucky to survive her ordeal. Despite the dreadful nature of her burns Miss Taylor's face remained unscathed. On arrival at the hospital she was attended to as well as possible by the medical staff, but their best efforts were not enough. She died on Wednesday 13 May.

An inquest was held the following day when a verdict of accidental death was recorded. Mr Jones, the young man who had tried so heroically to rescue the poor girl did not escape unhurt. His hands and arms had become so badly blistered in his gallant efforts that they had incapacitated him from his employment. Mr Jones firmly refused the generous offer of a reward made to him by Miss Taylor's employer, stating that he did not wish for any recognition.

A CYCLIST'S CLAIM

At the Birkenhead County Court on 26 February 1901 Judge Bowen Rowlands presided over an action for accidental damages. Lottie Hayward pressed charges against John Rohlederer for injuries caused to her through, what she claimed, was the reckless driving of one of his servants. Frederick Smith (later the Earl of Birkenhead) appeared for the plaintiff, whilst Mr A. Tobin acted on behalf of the defendant.

At the sitting Mr Smith stated that Miss Hayward was a young woman living in Bury who worked as a hotel waitress. The previous August, she and her mother had left the town and travelled to West Kirby for a short summer holiday. On the afternoon of 16 February, Lottie decided to go for a bicycle ride with the daughter of her hospitable landlady, Mrs Williams.

The pair rode out to Hoylake and spent the day talking and taking in the sights and charming scenery. Later, the two friends decided to return home, so they lit their bicycle lamps in preparation for navigating the dark and potentially hazardous roads.

Turning into Banks Road proved to be somewhat perilous; that road was quite sharp and steep, so the pair checked their lamps and proceeded slowly.

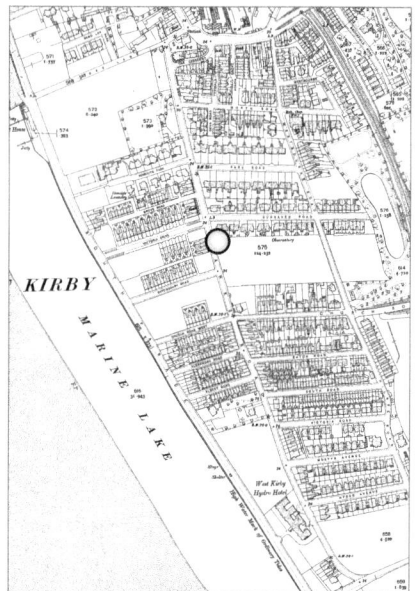

Banks Road, West Kirby, on a map dated 1911.

It was then, Mr Smith alleged, that the sound of a rapidly approaching vehicle came from nowhere and soon a landau driven by one of Mr Rohlederer's employees rushed upon them with great speed. The court heard how Edith Williams, the plaintiff's companion, was thrown from her bicycle onto the parapet under a shop window and sustained a twisted ankle. Miss Hayward herself was not so lucky. She was thrown down onto the road and before she could escape, a wheel of the horse-drawn carriage passed painfully over her foot. She was very much shaken by the incident and her stay at West Kirby lasted considerably longer than she had expected. Lottie was kept from her employment for six weeks due to the injury and was claiming £16 6d in compensation. Miss Williams corroborated this statement.

For the defence, Charles Lonnie stated that he had witnessed the incident and recalled that at the time of the accident he had been walking with his wife when he saw the landau. Three ladies were crossing the road, he said, and the driver of the cab shouted to them. Immediately afterwards Mr Lonnie recalled that the driver shouted a second time and upon hearing him, the witness noticed the two cyclists coming

Banks Road, West Kirby, as it looked in the early twentieth century.

along the crescent. One of them, he claimed, was in the middle of the road while the other was close to the footpath. The carriage driver was in the middle of the road, but slightly over to his proper side. He noticed that one of the females had become startled at the sudden sight of the horse and that she had begun to wobble, cutting across the landau's path. Charles stated that during this whole frightening affair the driver of the cab was pulling up all the time in an attempt to avoid any collisions. It seemed to him that there was sufficient space for the two riders to pass the vehicle on their proper side without any problems. Mrs Lonnie corroborated this statement.

With two opposing versions of events, Edward Talbot, the driver of the landau in question, was called to be questioned. He answered stating that his horse that evening was not capable of travelling any faster than 6 or 7mph, and at the time of the accident the equipage was certainly not travelling at full pace. Mr Talbot then said that he had first spotted the ladies when they were at about 10yds distance from his horse's nose. It was his firm opinion that at that time there was plenty of room for them both to pass him safely. On his approach he remembered that Miss Hayward began to wobble and veered into the centre of the road. This was at about 4 or 5yds distance, and it was at this point that Edward claimed he began halting his horse as fast as he possibly could. There was nothing more he could have done.

The defence solicitor contended that if his honour found his client guilty of negligence then the wobbling of Miss Hayward's bicycle into Mr Talbot's horse's path at the last moment, instead of pursuing the proper passage when there was clearly room, must prove that any negligence was totally on her part.

His honour Judge Rowlands thought that on the whole, the plaintiff was entitled to succeed in this matter. It seemed to him that there was a definite story told by the two ladies which was inconsistent with the case put forward for the defence. And besides, if there was sufficient time for the driver to observe the initial wobbling of the bicycle, then there was sufficient time for him to pull up and stop. Judgement was ruled for the plaintiff for the amount claimed.

THE NEW BRIGHTON BLAZE

In the year 1916, the Palace, a large and exciting entertainment venue, once stood proudly on New Brighton's famous promenade. This building was just one of the many attractions that Cheshire and Lancashire thrillseekers travelled far and wide to visit. Inside was an impressive motor car circular switchback, which by today's white-knuckle standards would be classed as a primitive rollercoaster. Alongside stood a variety of small side-shows which were all packed heavily with fancy goods in preparation for the upcoming Easter season.

On the morning of 22 April, PC Ryan was doing his rounds in the seaside town, walking along the prom. In the distance he spotted a truly ominous sight. A plume of thick black smoke was pouring from the Palace, and soon he observed the flickering flames of a fierce blaze.

The constable immediately contacted the fire brigade who soon arranged for two engines to be sent to the scene. Despite the swiftness of the firemen's response, the inferno had increased and was now igniting neighbouring properties. The contents of the buildings were of a highly inflammable nature and soon turned what should have been a house of fun into a dismally blackened, charred wreck.

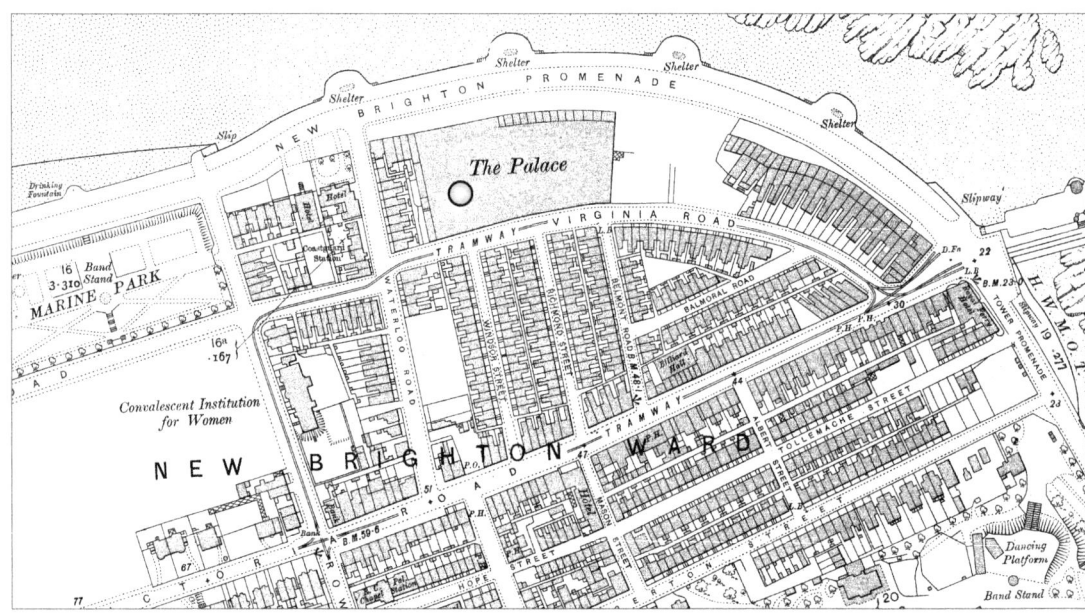

New Brighton as seen on a map from 1912.

The promendae at New Brighton, in the early twentieth century.

Fortunately no one was inside the building at that early hour; the only loss being of a material kind.

Firemen persisted in fighting new outbreaks of flames from the smouldering ruin and it was with great relief they were able to save the Gaiety Theatre and the nearby skating rink. However they were unable to rescue the six adjoining shops which had suffered the force of the fire's aggression. Huge chunks of masonry had crashed into the cellars, leaving behind a vista of grotesquely twisted iron girders and smouldering rubble. All that was left were a few portions of tottering walls which bore great cracks, and in the centre of this debris stood a solitary piece of iron chimney; the only remnants of the indoor rollercoaster.

The brigade remained locked in combat with the blaze for several hours before the servicemen successfully took control.

That weekend saw the surviving walls come tumbling down as crowds gathered to watch their final demolition. On the Sunday afternoon, a Liscard lad called Willie Jones, aged ten, was the youthful subject of a rather miraculous escape. During the pulling down of the brickwork, the boy, obviously a little too keen to watch, had found himself a rather dangerous vantage point. Before any warning could be given a huge mass of brickwork came crashing down upon him. The coastal spectators fully expected to see the boy crushed. All hearts were in mouths as the masonry fell silent and the dust cleared. Then, rising from the debris, they saw the boy. He had somehow escaped death, even injury, bar a slight gash on the nose. Astonished rescuers rushed over and soon the lucky youngster was on his way to the Borough Hospital to be treated for shock.

The destroyed building covered an area of between 150 and 200sq yds, most of which, if not all, belonged to the Corporation. The damage was estimated to run into thousands of pounds.

A LAMENTABLE LABOUR

In the year 1896 a truly heart-rending inquest took place at the Victoria Hotel, Cleveland Street, Birkenhead. Dr Henry Churton presided over the investigation into the death of thirty-three-year-old Johannah Allen, who before her tragic death lived at 22 Pool Street. On the night of Tuesday 18 April Mrs Allen went into labour. Dr Wilkinson was called for but the administration of chloroform proved useless. Later that night, both mother and child died.

The first witness called was Dr Dalzell, who told the court that he had carried out a thorough post-mortem on the deceased woman. He was accompanied by doctors Wilkinson and Stansfield, the former being present at the time of death.

Dr Dalzell explained that the body of Mrs Allen was generally very blanched, a condition that was caused by what seemed to him enormous blood loss. On investigating the abdomen the surgeon said he found it to be grossly inflated and in the most dependent portion, the peritoneum, there was only approximately 6oz of blood. There was also a rupture of about 4in, but this the doctor could not explain.

The coroner remarked that the case in question was quite extraordinary, and that he hoped that the medical men present that morning would take careful consideration and patience in explaining everything to himself and the jury.

An 1899 map showing Pool Street, Birkenhead.

Dr Dalzell continued, stating that the dead child was fully developed at nine months but, unusually, it had an exceptionally large head. The afterbirth, instead of being just that, was a forebirth and was in such a position that the baby could not be born without its prior removal. The doctor described how this was done, but not without considerable difficulty and immense blood loss.

'Now up to that point had you anything to indicate the cause of death?' Dr Churton asked.

'The main cause of death, I think, was a brain haemorrhage.' Replied Dr Dalzell.

'I suppose the case is an unusual one?' The coroner enquired. 'Did you ever see one before?'

'Yes, I have seen two. It is very unusual and very dangerous.'

The conversation continued, the coroner adamant that all his medical questions surrounding the deaths were answered succinctly.

'I suppose you have been in the profession a good many years?

'Since 1881.' Dr Dalzell replied. 'Fourteen years.'

'And I suppose all these irregularities, diseases, I may call them, must have caused a great deal of pain?

'A good deal of pain!'

'Suppose a person had seen her a few hours before her death and had operated upon her, would it be possible to think that she might have survived the operation?'

'I don't think so, sir'.

'Supposing you had given her some remedy yourself during her lifetime on finding her to be in such a state of agony, I may call it, and general pain, what might you have given to revive her?'

The doctor paused for a moment. 'I should have given her an anaesthetic, probably chloroform.'

'Did you find any other cause of death besides what you have described?

'No sir. The woman was very fat and stout.'

'Chest alright?'

'I did not think it was necessary to examine the chest.' Dr Dalzell answered. 'I found sufficient cause there.'

'Quite, I should think.' Dr Churton remarked. 'Can you form an opinion as to the probable amount of haemorrhage she might have suffered from?

'She must have lost a great deal of blood because the whole of the skin was blanched and there was no blood in any of the blood vessels. I did not notice any blood myself, but there must have been a very large quantity indeed, and the operation was one which if it is required to be done, must be done quickly.'

The coroner at this point stated that no more questions would be put to the witness. Dr Dalzell had given evidence most satisfactorily and he had explained the cause of death clearly.

Dr Churton began summing up the case.

'I think most of the gentlemen understand this woman died from haemorrhage caused by rupture inside as well as outside the womb, so that she must have lost a great deal of blood.'

The foreman remarked that he imagined all those present would be united in the opinion that all that could have been done to save Mrs Allen was done. The coroner declared that he fully agreed with those sentiments and allowed the jury ten minutes to finalise their decision. The foreman declined, affirming that the jury believed the evidence of Dr Dalzell made the matter perfectly clear.

Dr Churton commented that he was most glad to have heard such evidence as

Pool Street, Birkenhead, the scene of the fatal labour.

it entirely exonerated Dr Wilkinson or anyone else who might have been with the woman before her passing.

'I suppose you have nothing to say about this matter?' the coroner asked Dr Wilkinson. 'Have you ever attended her before?'

'No sir, not at all. I was called upon suddenly and she was dead within three hours of the time it commenced. She came out of the chloroform.'

'Well you gave what you thought was right to relieve her of the pain?'

'Yes.' Dr Wilkinson responded. 'It was not from the chloroform at all from which she died'.

The questions were suddenly cut short.

'We are quite satisfied it was not with the chloroform', the foreman interrupted.

'No blame is attributed to anybody in this case, to no professional man at any rate,' the coroner concluded.

The jury then returned a verdict of death from natural causes.

ANIMAL CRUELTY

Robert Sherlock was a sixty-two-year-old general porter who lodged at a house in Seagrave Street, Liverpool. On the afternoon of 20 March 1896, Mr Sherlock made his way to the Cheshire side of the Mersey to deliver a parcel to an address in New Ferry. This he did with the least of trouble and soon afterwards the elderly gentleman set off on his return journey back to Liverpool. As he walked through the town of New Ferry in the direction of Lower Bebington, Robert passed through a number of fields, one of which stood near the footpath situated on Old Chester Road, leading to Bebington Village. This plot of land contained a rather large donkey which stood idly grazing as Mr Sherlock slowly hobbled his way past.

Suddenly the once-docile donkey charged the old man at a frightful pace. It forced him to the ground, pinning its helpless victim down with its powerful forelegs. The horrendous attack left the man struggling as hard as his weak and feeble muscles

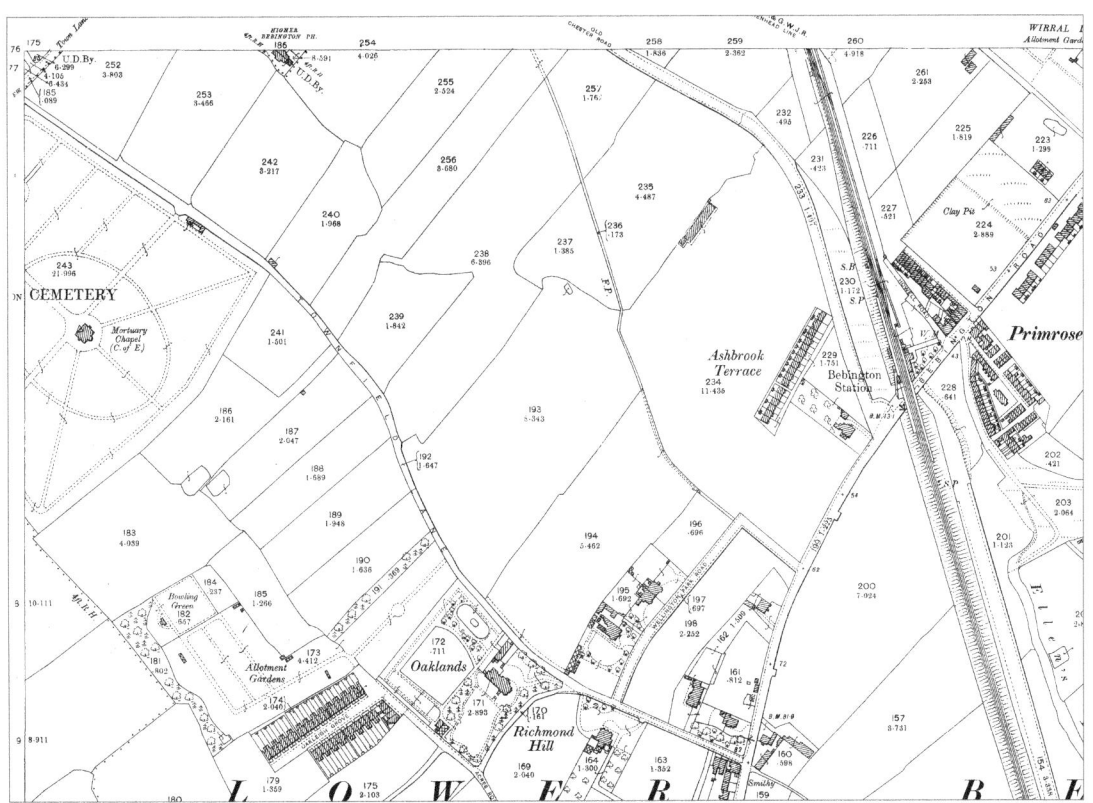

The vicinity of Old Chester Road in 1900.

could manage. Mr Sherlock aimed several firm blows at the donkey's underside and rear with his walking stick in a desperate bid for freedom. His retaliation merely served to further infuriate the animal, which began to butt Robert's face and neck and to bite viciously like a rabid dog. The man continued raining blows upon the donkey, which, after some sinister braying, relented, affording Mr Sherlock time to get up and slowly escape the crazed beast.

Sergeant William Burgess was on duty that afternoon when he spotted a bedraggled old man coming towards him. He listened to Mr Sherlock's account of the donkey's brutal and unprovoked attack. Robert told the officer that prior to his horrific experience he had noticed some lads throwing stones at the donkey, probably trying to madden the animal. He further stated that he had walked that route a dozen or more times and had never had any reason to complain about the animal before.

The officer made enquiries and discovered that the owner of the murderous donkey could be found at his nearby shop. Robert Benfield, fishmonger and poultry dealer of 62 New Chester Road, told Sergeant Burgess that he did indeed rent the land and as far as he knew the animal he kept there was usually quite docile. He himself used to offer rides on the donkey to local children, including his own daughter. The trader was most upset at the awful incident and offered Mr Sherlock some brandy and pledged to pay any medical expenses that he may incur.

Parting on good terms, Mr Sherlock was taken back home to Liverpool. He had never married and had no remaining living relatives. His only companion was his landlady who kindly tended his wounds while listening to his account.

'If I had not struck the animal across the legs I would have been killed by it!' Robert exclaimed.

His condition worsened overnight and the following morning Mr Sherlock was forced to be admitted to the Brownlow Hill Workhouse Hospital.

Dr Clapham examined the man and found the patient to be suffering from shock. There was a wound on his head, about 5in long, which showed no sign of healing. Robert was forced to keep to his bed due to his condition which grew steadily worse. On 18 April he developed bronchitis which soon spread to his lungs. Robert died the following week from bronchopneumonia accelerated by injuries to the head.

An inquest was held by the Liverpool City Coroner, Mr Sampson on 29 April. He addressed the jury by saying that owners should be most careful about animals they kept in public places. The public have a right to pass with ordinary safety through any public place. If a man knew an animal to be vicious, he would be held civilly responsible for any injuries that it caused.

A verdict in accordance with the medical testimony was returned. The donkey's fate is unknown.

A LETHAL TOY

On 14 November 1881 PC Fairhurst was walking his beat along Price Street, Birkenhead, when he was abruptly accosted by a hysterical local woman. She informed the constable that a boy had just been shot dead in Maddock Street and that he should come to the scene at once. He hurried around to the property at No. 4, where he discovered the body of a young male lying dead in the hallway. The corpse lay bleeding from the left eye and temple, and the entire face appeared rather blackened. The body, which was established to be that of twelve-year-old Joseph Fernley, was sent to the Borough Hospital for examination. PC Fairhurst commenced a search of the house and almost immediately discovered a gun lying on the floor just inside the doorway. There was no doubt that this was the weapon that had killed young Joe.

Elsewhere in Lydia Terrace, PC Cunningham had been informed of the killing and had arrested an alleged suspect. He had charged eight-year-old John Ingley with causing the death of Master Fernley and the prisoner was remanded. On hearing the charge against him John made a rambling statement which neither PC Cunningham nor any of his colleagues could comprehend. Despite his severe form of special needs John was taken to the cells to await trial.

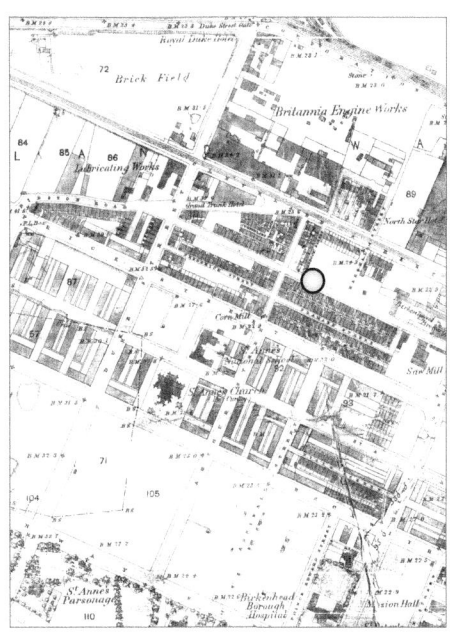

Maddock Street on a map dating from 1876.

The following Tuesday Henry Churton, Borough Coroner, held an inquest at the Queens Hotel into young Joseph Fernley's death.

Mary Broadfield, wife of James Broadfield, deposed that she was the elder sister of John Ingley. She claimed that when she had left the house in Maddock Street on the morning of the death she had told James to let her know when the landlord came round. Mary stated that there was a gun in the house. It was loaded, but not capped. She said that on returning home at about two o'clock, she had, to her horror, found the door pane to be smeared with blood and the gun in the hallway.

'He's not all there.' Mary confessed, before relating that John's mental problems prevented him from receiving a proper schooling.

When questioned Francis Griffiths answered that he had been in the vicinity of Maddock Street on his way home for dinner. He had heard a gunshot emanate from

A modern view of the remaining part of Maddock Street.

the Broadfield house and at once ran over. There the witness had watched as Ingley had thrown down the gun, run out of the building and down the street. 'Oh father, I've killed Joe! I'll go get drowned!' Francis heard the lad cry, as he fled towards the docks.

Emma Fernley, mother of the victim, told the court that her son had left their home in Lydia Terrace at about twenty minutes to two on the afternoon of his death. Shortly afterwards, Mrs Fernley claimed to have heard the distinct sound of a gun. She ran out of the house and round to Mrs Broadfield's, where upon arrival she was greeted with the appalling scene of death. Emma fought back tears, saying that the prisoner and her boy had always been on the best of terms. However, she thought that it was worthwhile to mention that John had been injured on a tram sometime ago and it appeared to her that he had never been quite the same since.

Dr Bernstein of the Borough Hospital deposed that the body of the deceased was brought to him on the Monday afternoon. On examining it he had found a gunshot wound external to the left eye. The shot had entered the skull and penetrated into the brain. The hair on the left side of the head had been singed and charred. The doctor deduced that the gun must have been fired at an extremely close range.

John Ingley was next to be interrogated. He coyly replied saying he had found the gun and was showing it to Joseph when the accident occurred. He said that neither of them thought it was loaded but that he had carelessly put a lighted match to the nipple while his friend was looking down the muzzle. The trigger was pulled, the gun went off and Fernley slumped down dead; the bullet burrowed deep inside his head.

The coroner remarked that as far as he could learn the two boys had always been companions and the best of friends, and in fact had merely been playing together with the firearm, not knowing that it was loaded, when the fatality took place. Mr Churton commented strongly on the stupidity of people who could leave a loaded gun in a place where it could be found by two such boys. He considered it a most careless proceeding on the part of the Broadfields.

The jury, after consulting for several moments, returned an open verdict.

John Ingley's ordeal was not over. He was brought before magistrate Mr Preston two days later and the evidence of the case was formally reheard, before the boy's fate was finally decided.

Mr Preston condemned the Broadfields for leaving a loaded gun in such an unintelligent manner where it could, and so easily was, got hold of by two small children, one so obviously an imbecile. The magistrate trusted that the death of Joseph Fernley would be a harsh lesson to all persons in the future. He did not believe that there was any felonious intent on the part of the prisoner and ordered John to be discharged.

OVEREXCITED

In the early morning of 26 March 1896 twelve-year-old Elsie James awoke from her sleep. The girl got up, dressed and quietly tiptoed down the staircase at the house in Blucher Street, Tranmere. She made her way into the kitchen and prepared breakfast, not only for herself, but also for her family who were still sound asleep upstairs. Elsie was feeling most excited after receiving a new score to play on the piano the previous evening and she was eager to attempt it that very moment. The youngster quickly gobbled down her breakfast and hurried over to sit at the family's large piano, where she began practising the rhythmical notes.

Not long afterwards Elsie's family, who were no doubt awoken by the music, left their beds and came to see what Elsie was doing playing the piano at such an early hour that Thursday morning.

'Elsie!' her mother called out. The music had suddenly stopped.

'Elsie!' the cry was repeated. Again there was no answer.

Blucher Street as seen on a map dated 1899.

Mrs James made her way into the parlour where she was surprised to see her daughter lying on the floor, apparently asleep. Elsie's mother attempted to wake her, but the girl could not be roused. This was much more than a nap.

Dr Ernest Woodey was contacted and arrived with his equipment about fifteen minutes later. It was his sad duty to inform the family that Elsie's life was already extinct.

Coroner Churton held an inquest at the Royal Standard Hotel the following Tuesday. Dr Woodey was the first witness to be questioned. He told the court that that he could not recall treating the deceased before and that if he had it would not have been for anything serious. The doctor stated that he had made a post-mortem examination of the body forty-eight hours after death and found the heart and lungs to be quite healthy with no sign of disease being present. The witness had examined Elsie's stomach and found that it contained about three ounces of partially digested food, bread he thought, but there was no sign of any inflammation on the wall of the stomach; which was perfectly healthy. The liver and kidneys were in the same impeccable condition.

'How was the spleen?' Dr Churton enquired.

'It was all right.'

'Were the glands all right?'

'Yes, the mesenteric glands were not inflamed at all.' Dr Woodey replied.

Continuing, the doctor related how he opened the girl's skull and examined its glutinous contents. He said that he had discovered the membranes to be perfectly fine but Elsie James' blood vessels were enormously congested; even the finest arteries were double or in some extreme cases, treble their normal size. There was no sign of any accumulation of blood in the ventricles. Dr Woodey exclaimed that in all his life he had never seen a brain so full of blood!

'What in your opinion caused the suddenness of death?' Dr Churton put to the witness.

'I think that in all probability it was caused by the sudden enormous congestion of the brain, probably due to some vasomotor disturbance affecting the blood vessels.'

The court mused solemnly over the reply.

'Was there no external bleeding from the head at all?'

'None whatsoever'

'Have you ever met with such a case before?' the coroner asked.

Dr Woodey took a moment to think.

'One, I think. You held an inquest relative to it yourself, remember?'

The coroner sighed.

'I cannot remember.'

'Wasn't it onboard the *Akbar*?' Dr Woodey persisted, 'Some four years ago?'

Dr Churton told the witness that his memory would not carry him so far back. He gruffly explained that he had such a vast number of cases to deal with each and every year that with every new one he soon forgot the last.

Getting back to the case, Dr Churton probed further into the matter with a new question.

'Have you ever made a post-mortem without finding out the cause of death?'

'No', answered Dr Woodey sternly.

The coroner's memory suddenly came back to him

'Well I saw one a few months ago just beyond Nantwich, where the body was examined head to foot and nothing was found. No account could be given of any disease of any structure whatsoever.'

The doctor agreed, and said that he could quite understand such an occurrence, but in this case there was no doubt that the cause of Elsie James's untimely death was sudden congestion of the brain. Her blood vessels were simply engorged! The witness related that he had sliced open her brain in several directions but could find no form of haemorrhage at all and nothing appeared to be out of the ordinary.

Mrs Margaret James, the deceased's mother, was next to be questioned. She informed the court that her daughter had bread and marmalade for breakfast, as was normal.

'Had she ever complained of headache?' Dr Churton asked.

'No, sir.'

She went onto confirm that on the morning of her death, Elsie had arisen from bed, taken breakfast and had began playing a new piece of music in the parlour. Mrs James then tearfully recounted how she had found her daughter dead upon the floor.

The coroner said that it seemed a very strange thing that all the substance of the brain, the veins, the membranes and arteries were in such a state of unaccountable congestion. It was a most unnatural occurrence.

'It is sometimes produced by excitement, according to Doctor Gowers, who I suppose is a leading authority.' answered Dr Woodey.

In response, the coroner stated that the deceased was evidently labouring under some intense excitement when playing at the piano. It was one of the most extraordinary cases he had ever had to preside over; in fact, he remarked that he had never seen anything quite like it. In summing up, Dr Churton stated that in his opinion the highly congested state of the brain arising from natural causes brought about Elise's end. The jury concurred and returned a verdict of death from natural causes.

MORTAL ELEVATION

Teenager John Francis Brown, of 17 Field Street, Birkenhead, set off for work bright and early on the morning of 4 January 1913. The fourteen-year-old had left school only the previous week and was eager to get to grips with his new job as a bottle boy for the Hamilton Street firm, Mackie and Gladstone.

Later that day John was busily engaged in cleaning a floor on one of the upper levels of the manufactory. Another employee, Thomas Hurley, escorted two lads upstairs to help John with his task, before leaving the boys to finish the job unsupervised. Shortly afterwards, labourer William Carey was in the middle of trucking some stout to various locations about the factory on the ground floor. Once he had a truckload of barrels ready to be taken to the top floor, he made his way over to the lift intending to send it up to his colleagues above. William approached the lift but found that it was in use so shook the rope from side to side hoping to attract the attention of whoever was using it.

'How long are you going to be?' Mr Carey shouted up.

'Wait a minute!' came the immediate and somewhat high-pitched reply.

Suddenly the electric elevator began to move and almost at once the same voice screamed out in heart-stopping agony.

From upstairs Mr Hurley heard the commotion and ran over to the origin of the outcry, the lift. Little John Brown was trapped. His legs were dangling down the shaft while his torso was wedged firmly under the imposing iron girder which ran across the top of the lift.

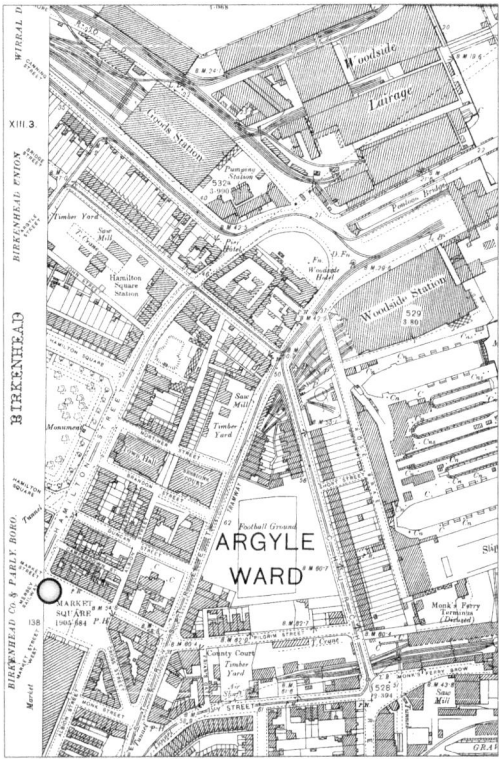

Hamilton Street on a map dated 1911.

'Stop the lift!' Thomas ordered. The whole workforce stopped and gathered around to help the boy down from his unenviable position. An ambulance was called for and John was hurried to the Borough Hospital where he was treated by Dr Allen. The sheer force of the accident had caused the youth's body to rupture internally and he died the following day. Death was due to generalised peritonitis, the result of injuries to the abdomen.

MORTAL ELEVATION

The Mackie & Gladstone factory, c. 1900.

A number of witness statements regarding the lift were heard at the inquest conducted by Mr Cotton on the following Wednesday.

Henry Foster, foreman bottler at Messrs Mackie and Gladstone, stated that when the guard gate of the lift went out of order he would wedge it down so that it could not be used. He habitually warned the factory boys to keep off the lift altogether, but he had not had a chance to warn his most recent worker, John Francis Brown.

Mr McNier, His Majesty's Inspector of Factories, told the court that he had visited the works and had no complaints to make. The fencing around the doors was in good order and everything was in accordance with government requirements.

It was clear that the whole incident was one of the utmost misfortune. The jury returned a verdict of accidental death, adding that they attached no blame to anyone whatsoever. They expressed deep sympathy with the deceased's relatives

A DAY AT THE RACES

On the afternoon of 23 May 1880 the Wirral Agricultural Society played host to its popular variety show at their grounds near to the Docks station, Birkenhead. It was the Whit Monday holiday and Mary Johnson, a sixty-five-year-old resident of Claughton Road, left her home to attend the spectacle, which she had been looking forward to for some time. Mrs Johnson was particularly keen to watch the horse racing, as were the six to seven thousand other spectators who had travelled from far and wide to witness the event. The course was oval in shape and of a substantial size; it was certainly large enough to race up to ten horses at any one time. The elderly woman watched the day's proceedings joyously until the show began to draw to a close late in the afternoon. At about half-past four, the fifth and final race of the day came under starter's orders. Mary was sitting on the ground with her legs projecting beneath the 4ft high safety fence. She had secured herself a prime spot to get the best views of the runners and riders as they prepared to race

An 1876 map showing Claughton Road, Oxton.

around the track. PC Price warned Mrs Johnson about the dangers of sitting so close to the course. In fact, he warned her several times but on each occasion the stubborn old woman refused to listen. PC Price could not physically remove her; besides, he already had enough to contend with as numerous careless individuals began straying onto the course. He was one of only eleven constables on duty at the event and a mere twenty-five stewards provided their only additional assistance in keeping order among the mammoth crowds.

Suddenly a huge cry went up. The horses were off and the crowd began roaring their encouragement at the racers as they galloped hard to get a strong lead. They sped their way round the course for about half a mile before Mary spotted them drawing nearer. As she sat under the rail, the old woman shouted and cheered the riders as loudly as her frail lungs could manage. They sped closer and closer and it seemed that all was going well. Two jockeys however became a little too eager and soon the merry cries of the onlookers became a collective intake of breath. The two men lost control of their steeds and crashed heavily into each other. One breathless equine was sent crashing into the safety rail, coming to a sudden halt with great violence. Mrs Johnson was terrified. If it had not been for the barrier she would have been crushed under the beast's enormous weight. The horse was uninjured but in its haste to get to its feet began kicking out erratically. In its struggle the horse struck the unfortunate Mrs Johnson who had so narrowly avoided death only seconds before. She was knocked flat to the ground as the animal's heavy metal shoe repeatedly struck her lower body.

The mount charged off, riderless, down the track, leaving PC Price, a number of stewards and fellow spectators to attend to the injured lady.

She was soon conveyed to the Borough Hospital whereupon arrival she was treated by Dr Baker, a house surgeon. The doctor found her to be in a severe state of shock due to her painful physical injuries. Her lower thigh was broken and her left leg had become dislocated. This was also badly bruised and Mrs Johnson's right hand was also wounded.

On the following Wednesday an unfavourable change took place in her condition and the elderly woman's state of health began to deteriorate. Four days later, Mary Johnson was dead. She died at quarter-past-six on the Sunday evening. Death was due to exhaustion. A jury at a subsequent inquest held at the Ranelagh Hotel returned a verdict of accidental death.

THE DANGERS OF NAPTHA

On 19 February 1887 an accident of an exceptionally painful character was incurred by the unfortunate Taylor family at their humble home in Tranmere. Inside a small hut situated in a field at the bottom of Willmer Road lived the family of Edward Taylor. Inside the property that Friday evening was Mr Taylor's children, Joseph and Hannah, his mother-in-law Sarah Hughes and his sister-in-law Ellen. Mrs Hughes was busily engaged in some ironing and her two young grandchildren sat playing on the floor. Tragically and without warning, the glowing naptha lamp which was suspended from the ceiling ignited, sending flaming-hot embers upon the children below. Mrs Hughes at once began suppressing the flames, but not before the siblings had sustained serious injury. Sarah herself caught alight as she attempted to remove the oil lamp from the property and out

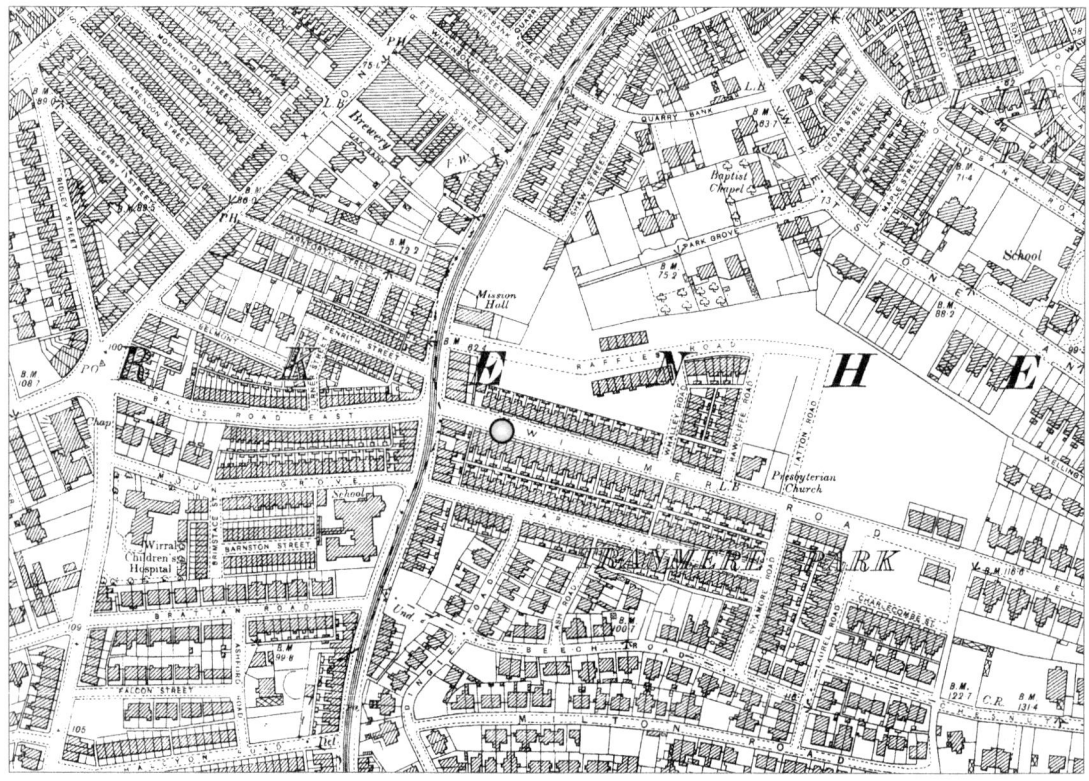

The vicinity of Willmer Road and Borough Road on a map dated 1899.

The junction of Willmer Road and Borough Road, 2007.

into the darkened street. Her screams were heard by Mrs M'Lay from her home at 66 Whetstone Lane. At about nine o'clock, Mr M'Lay, on the frenetic guidance of his wife, ran around to the origin of the outcry to find the shack ablaze. He at once returned to inform his wife of what he had seen and the couple immediately went back to aid the suffering family. The house was full of smoke and Mrs Hughes cradled the eighteen-month baby and the four-year-old toddler in her reddened arms at the doorstep. Mrs M'Lay took Hannah, who was screaming in distress, from Sarah and saw to her wounds. The two juveniles were soon taken to the Children's Hospital and Mrs Hughes to the Borough Hospital where they were each treated for burns. Hannah sadly passed away the following Saturday morning.

An inquest was held by Mr Churton into the child's death on Monday 22 February. Mrs Taylor, mother of the deceased, stated that she had only left the house a short time before she heard the screams. She said that she at once ran back to find her home alight and her family badly burnt. Miss Ellen Hughes was called to give evidence but during inquiries news was learnt that her mother Sarah had passed away. Ellen was so overwhelmed with grief that she could not stand. The coroner mercifully allowed her to leave the proceedings to grieve her loss.

The jury in returning a verdict of accidental death, expressed that the use of such naptha lamps in the presence of children was most ill-advised. An inquest into the death of the forty-six-year-old was held the following day. Mr Churton read over the previous day's evidence and asked the witnesses if they had anything else to add. They did not, and a second verdict of accidental death was accordingly returned.

LOADED

On the evening of Monday 25 May 1896 a large collection of men gathered in the back parlour of the Pacific Hotel in Price Street, Birkenhead. The time was about nine o'clock and the party of approximately twenty individuals took their seats and ordered some drinks. The crowd was quite cheerful and they chatted and laughed as they sipped their pints in the warm and cosy atmosphere.

The licensee of the well-known establishment was George Foulkes. About five years previously, Mr Foulkes had purchased three or four old Crimean War rifles as curiosities for his pub. He had never actually got around to displaying the antique weapons and they had been left to sit in an old upstairs lumber room. However the previous week the landlord had grew tired of the pieces and he had decided to get rid of them, placing the guns in a stable attached to the rear of the property. Somehow or other, the guns found their way into the busy back parlour.

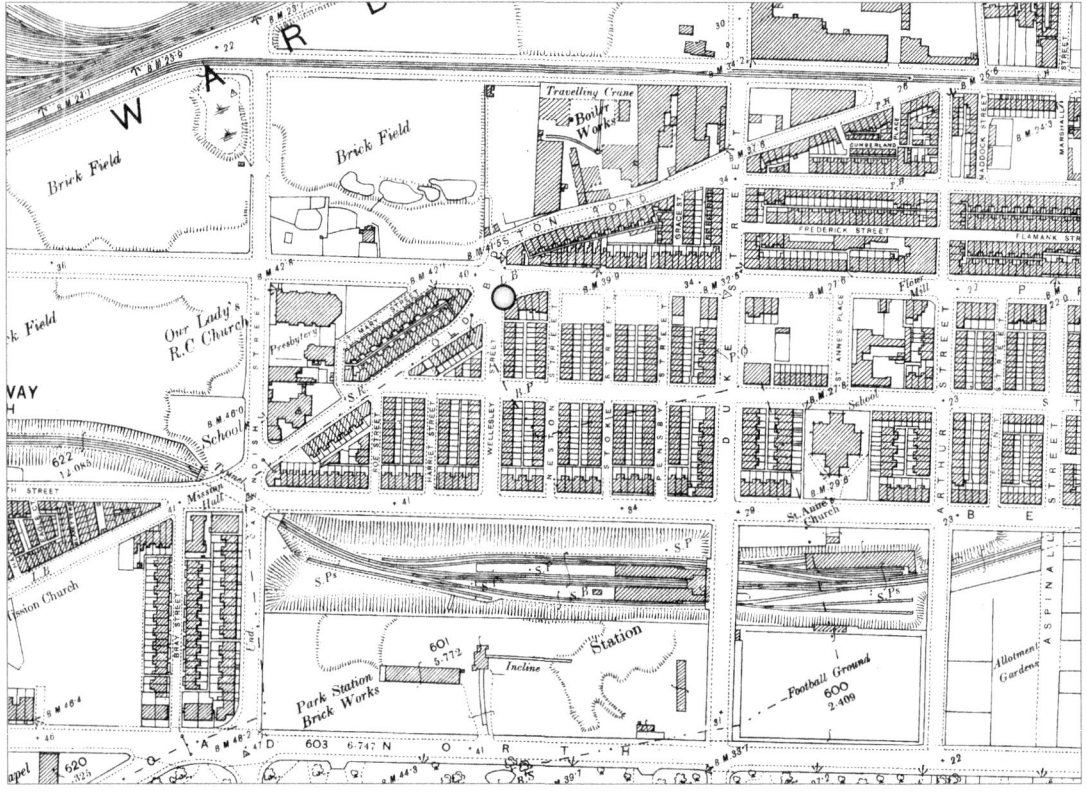

The Pacific Hotel on the corner of Old Bidston Road and Price Street in 1899.

Patrick Gray gleamed with delight at seeing the weapons. He had been in the army, serving in Egypt, and knew a great deal about various firearms. He took hold of one of the rifles and proceeded to play out a drill, taking on the role of instructor and informing his drinking pals how to load, aim and fire, stamping their feet as they did so. Everyone was laughing and joking as each man was passed a gun and tried their hand at being a soldier. The slightly inebriated Mr Gray began to get a little carried away with the fun. With the rifle resting between his knees, Patrick took out a Lucifer match, lit it and placed the flame to the nipple of the rifle.

'I'll be the first man to be shot!' joked Thomas Taggart, another member of the group. Gray happily obliged and pulled the trigger. Surprisingly the rifle fired; first the brimstone then the barrel before the whole room fell into a deadly silence.

Mr Foulkes's heart was pounding like never before. He had only moments before entered the room to serve a customer and had avoided being shot by a mere 6in! Taggart was not so fortunate. The newsagent had been in Gray's line of fire and had bore the full force of the blast. The bullet pierced his cheek and travelled right through the back of his neck before finally coming to a halt in the plasterwork behind him. Taggart fell backwards at Foulkes's feet. Blood began to steadily ooze from the blackened hole in his face causing all who witnessed the gruesome spectacle to immediately sober up.

'My God is he shot?' a now rather pale Patrick Gray asked. He suddenly realised what he had done. 'Oh my good God!' he murmured slowly.

An ambulance was called for but Mr Taggart died on the way to hospital.

Mr Gray was advised to make his way to the North End Bridewell and turn himself in. He left the pub and nervously walked around to the station where he confessed to the officer on duty of the evening's terrible goings-on. Detective Officer Hall cautioned Patrick and charged him with causing the death of Thomas Taggart. 'I did not know the rifle was loaded!' Gray pleaded, as he was remanded for the inevitable enquiries.

On Wednesday 27 May an inquest was held into the death at the Queens Hotel, Park Entrance.

The owner of the Pacific Hotel, Mr Foulkes, was the first to be questioned. He stated that he had known Mr Taggart for just over a year and knew he liked to have a drop or two to drink. He stated that he had seen him enter his pub at about twenty-to-nine and sit with some fellows who were already seated in the back parlour.

'You are the owner of the musket?' Dr Churton asked.

'Yes'.

'When did you last use it?'

'I have never used it', George replied. 'I bought three or four of them over five years ago as curiosities.'

Continuing, the witness stated that all the men present that night were quite sober and were all on friendly terms.

'You had a very fortunate escape yourself', the coroner added.

The Pacific Hotel, 2007.

'Yes!' George said with relief. 'If I had made one step further it would have gone through me instead of him!'

The coroner soon concluded his questions to the landlord. He remarked, however, that he could not understand why Mr Foulkes, a man of some age and experience, allowed the rifles to be on his premises for such a length of time without examining them.

Junior house surgeon at the Borough Hospital, Dr Henry Elliot, was next to be questioned. He had conducted a post-mortem upon the body the previous day and was asked to submit his findings. He said that he had observed a 2in wound, blackened and jagged at the edges, at the left side of the deceased's mouth which continued through to the rear of the neck. The jaw was shattered and some large blood vessels, along with the jugular vein, were ruptured. It was Dr Elliot's professional opinion that death was no doubt due to the bullet wound. The brain and spine were left unharmed and all of the other internal organs were in a perfectly healthy state.

Dr Churton remarked that the cause of death was as clear as possible. He believed it not to be a case of murder, but asked the jury to consider whether a verdict of manslaughter would be appropriate. The distinction lay in the fact as to whether there was malice.

The jury convened in private and later returned with a unanimous verdict. 'A purely accidental death', the foreman announced.

Nevertheless, with the local constabulary involved who maintained a view of possible manslaughter, Patrick Gray had yet to face Mr Gostenhofer at the Borough Police Court the following Friday.

Mr Reinhardt, on behalf of the prosecution stated that there was no deliberate intent on the part of the prisoner to kill or in any way injure Mr Taggart, but he did say that the use of dangerous weapons in the manner in which resulted in such a tragic occurrence was most careless. Mr Gray has every opportunity to examine the rifle that killed Thomas. There was a ramrod attached, and when the barrel was empty this fitted perfectly. The prosecution argued that if the accused had only checked he would have noticed that the ramrod was protruding by an inch or so. Indeed, such negligence, Mr Reinhardt argued, could only result in one verdict, a verdict of manslaughter. The inquest verdict was superficial.

The magistrate listened carefully to the evidence put before him. Mr Gostenhofer had been convinced and he considered that there was sufficient proof for Patrick Gray to be sent for further trial.

On 18 June the thirty-three-year-old was brought before Mr Justice Wright at the Chester Assizes. Subsequently, his Lordship remarked that had read through all the depositions of the case and could not find any evidence of criminal negligence on the part of the prisoner. It was certainly a most lamentable accident and it was most unadvisable for anyone to handle a firearm without prior examination. However the judge was clear in his view that he could not describe such neglect as criminal negligence. It was neither the view of a fellow judge, of whom he had consulted opinion upon the matter. 'I think he is entirely free from fault in the affair', said Mr Justice Wright as he reiterated his belief that it was just an innocent accident. The jury, on his lordship's direction, acquitted Patrick Gray of all charges.

No doubt the ex-soldier would show considerable more care when handling potentially lethal guns for the rest of his days.

UNDERTAKEN

On the wet afternoon of 3 June 1896 a sombre crowd descended upon Liverpool's Anfield cemetery. That Wednesday was to witness the funeral of the elderly Susan McFarlane, formerly of Red House, Upton, who had recently passed away. Her body lay solemnly in a wooden casket which was surrounded by tearful friends and relatives who had come to pay their last respects. Among them was undertaker John Howson Smith. He worked for the Birkenhead firm Messrs Higgins and Smith, and was at the graveside gently lowering the coffin into the ground. As he gripped tightly to the rope allowing him and his colleagues to lower the deceased steadily, Mr Smith suddenly came over rather ill.

He became breathless and was forced to relinquish his grasp of the line. The coffin fell, as did Mr Smith. He collapsed backwards and slowly slid down a tombstone of

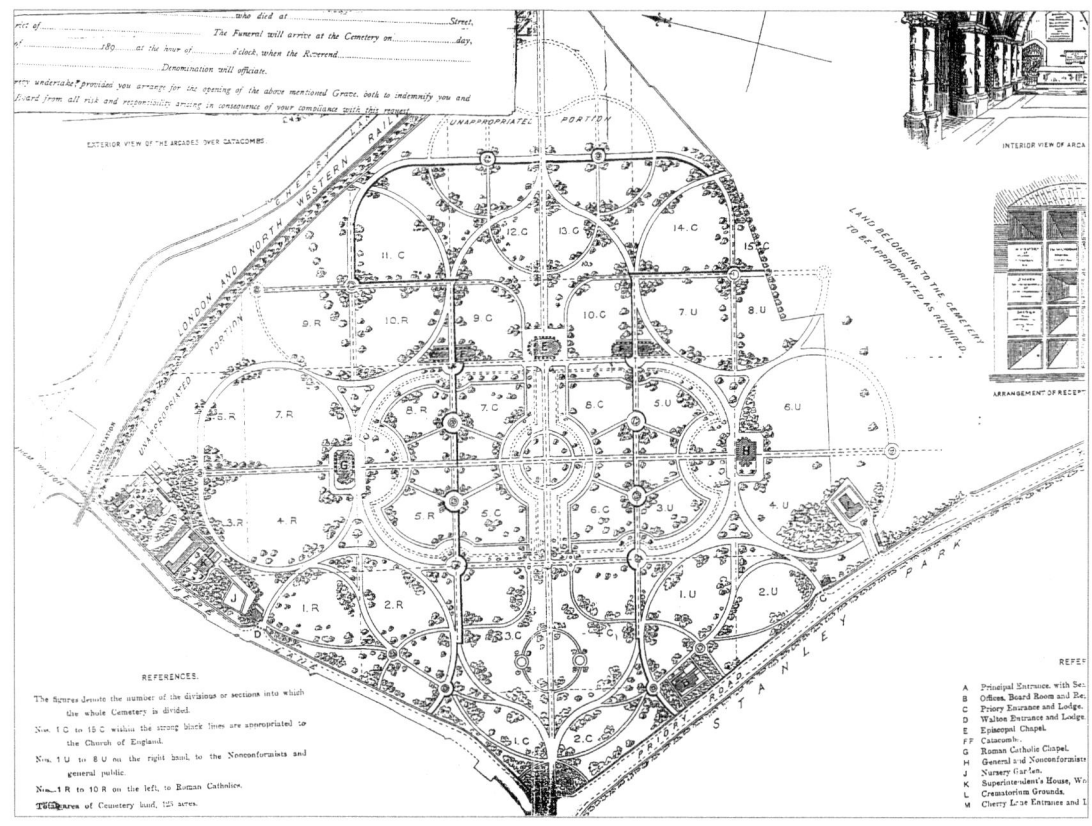

Anfield Cemetery in the nineteenth century.

which he had desperately lunged towards for support. Gasps were heard all around and the funeral was brought to an immediate and unplanned stop.

'I need a drink of water', John wheezed, as he was helped to his feet by fellow undertakers Mr Hogg and Mr Abbot.

He managed to stand and was slowly led to a seat. Mr Smith, on recovering his composure, said that he had felt as if he had been sleeping and before he knew it he was struggling to stay upright.

The funeral was soon back underway and the remaining undertakers stood silently, heads bowed, as the clergyman read out the remaining verses.

A few moments of grief passed before Mr Smith once again attracted the attention of mourners.

'In the midst of life we are in death', said the vicar, and with that, Mr Smith's head fell back and a vacant gaze fell upon his face. The woeful crowd turned to see what had happened and called out to the inert undertaker.

With no response, the seemingly lifeless man was placed into a mourning brougham and taken to the nearest doctor. On arrival it was found that no medicine could possibly save the man. He had died at the funeral.

An inquest was held the next day before Mr Sampson, Liverpool coroner. It was stated that earlier that afternoon the deceased was caught in a shower of rain and in order to escape getting wet, Mr Smith had run smartly to the cemetery office. It was believed that this exertion, along with his already debilitating muscular rheumatism, ultimately led to his premature end. The forty-three-year-old left behind a widow and several children. He was described to have had a most kind and genial nature, and was a man who would be sorely missed.

Death was attributed to the extra exertion of a weak heart and a verdict of death from natural causes was returned.

INDEX

Abbot, Mr 125
Allen, Dr 66, 114
Allen, Johannah 104, 105
Allen, Miss 77
Allen, Mr 18
Alton Road 77, 78
Anfield Cemetery 124
Angel Hotel 90
Argyle Street 13, 14, 17, 41
Argyle Street South 54
Ashby, Colonel 73
Ashcroft, Private 74
Astbury, Mrs 99

Baker, Dr 117
Banks, Percy 27, 28
Banks Road 100 101
Batchelor, Annie 50, 51
Batchelor, George 50
Batchelor, Hilda 50, 51
Bate, Mr J.C. 38, 96, 98
Bates, Mr 53, 56
Beal, Lance-Corporal 74
Beardwood, Captain and Adjutant 73, 74
Bebington Inspector 49
Bebington Showgrounds 71
Bedford Road 67, 68, 69
Beeston, Thomas 91, 92
Bell, Phillip 59, 60
Bell, Thomas 59, 60
Benfield, Robert 108
Bentley, Dr 73
Bernstein, Dr 110
Berry, Dr 80
Birkenhead Park 65
Bishop, J. 21
Bishop, Sarah 21, 22
Blucher Street 111
Booth, Mr 22
Borough Road 61, 94

Botham, Frederick 96
Bowman, Sergeant Edward 82
Brandon Street 54
Broadfield, James 109
Broadfield, Mary 109
Brooks, Thomas 47, 48, 49
Brougham Road 34
Brown, Dr 40
Brown, Francis 63
Brown, John Francis 114, 115
Brown, Revd Mr 90
Brownlow Road 95
Burge, Inspector 41
Burgess, William Sergeant 108
Burns, Superintendent 76

Calderbank, James 64
Campbell, Frederick 59, 60
Carey, William 114
Carruthers, Dr 46
Cavendish Drive 84, 85
Cearns Road 77, 78
Central station 71
Chester Street 17, 19, 47
Chestnut Grove 9, 10, 11
Chetwynd Road 77
Chevalier, Mr 85
Church Road 54
Church Street 17
Churton, Dr Henry 10, 12, 22, 46, 88, 90, 92, 104, 105, 106, 109, 110, 112, 113, 119, 121, 122
Clapham, Dr 108
Clarke, John 95
Clarke, Reggie 36, 37
Clarke, Thomas 36, 37
Claughton Road 116

Clavey, Dora 9, 10, 11, 12
Clavey, Frederick 9, 10
Clayton, Mr 17
Collins, Sarah 24
Connor, Private 73, 74
Conway Street 65
Cook, Dr 24
Cook, Mayor Alderman Thomas 53
Corniche Road 97
Cotton, Mr A.F. 85, 115
Coultard Road 35
Cowper, Mary Ann 25, 26
Crawley, James 62, 63
Crawshaw, PC 49
Cretin, Mr 58
Croft, Corporal 74
Cullen, Archibald 80
Cumberland Road 35
Cunningham, PC 109
Cust, Hon. Sir Edward 91

Dalzell, Dr 104, 105
Davies, Chief Constable 53
Demesne Street 34, 35
Denbigh Castle 47
Denson, John 54
Derby Road 10, 29
Derbyshire, Bessie 27, 28
Dickinson, George Edward 97
Dixon, Dr J. 51
Dodwell, William 19
Doolan, Private 74
Downham Road 71
Downing, Mr 89
Downs, Samuel 91
Duncan Street 54
Dyer, Private 72

INDEX

Elliot, Dr Henry 122
Ellis, Ann 90
Ellsworth, Amelia 23, 24
Ellsworth, Christopher 23, 24
Elm Grove 10
Elmswood Road 71
Entwistle, Private 74
Evans, Robert Daniel 10, 11

Fairclough Lane 86, 87
Fairhurst, PC 109
Famery, Superintendent 75
Feathers Inn 47
Ferguson, George 59, 60
Fermley, Emma 110
Fermley, Joseph 109, 110
Field Street 114
Finnegan, Mr 18
Flanagan, John 45, 46
Foster, Henry 115
Foulkes, George 120, 121, 122

Gardiner, George 34
Garrett, PC 63
Garrett, Percy 61
Gaskill, Annie 65
Godden, Mr 88
Godwin, Thomas 91
Gostenhofer, Mr 123
Gowers, Dr 113
Gray, Patrick 121, 123
Greenway Road 10, 11
Griffiths, Francis 109
Griffiths, PC 80

Haines, Hilda 32
Hall, Detective Officer 121
Hall, Henry Sproston 45, 46
Hamilton Square 52, 54, 77
Hamilton Street 13, 17, 54, 114
Hammond, Miss 43
Hare, Dr 64
Harris, Dr 43
Hartnup, John 43, 44
Harwood, Mr 90

Hayes, Mr 26
Hayward, Lottie 100, 101
Helmingham Road 30
Hepburn, Isabella 34, 35
Highfield Road 71
Hogg, Mr 125
Holden, Cecil 33, 69, 81, 94
Holt Hill 54
Holt Road 32
Hope Street 64
Hornblower, Major 88
Houghton, Private 74
Hughes, Ellen 118
Hughes, Jabez 40
Hughes, John 93, 94
Hughes, Sarah 118, 119
Humphrey, Thomas 92
Hunt, Joshua 47, 48, 49
Hurley, Thomas 114

Ingley, John 109, 110

Jackson, Sergeant 95
James, Elsie 111, 112, 113
James, Mrs 112
Johnson, Abel 86, 87, 88
Johnson, Charles 86, 87, 88
Johnson, Harriet 88
Johnson, Mary 116, 117
Johnson, Samuel 88
Johnston, Dr William 10
Jones, Mr 99
Jones, Mrs 93, 94
Jones, Willie 103

Kane, Ellen 89
Kane, James 90
Kay, Mr 13
Kemp, Alfred 37
King Street 29, 74
Kings Lane 45

Laird, John 53
Lally, Private 74
Lambert, Dr 31
Langley, Bertram 84, 85
Langley, Mrs 84, 85
Larchwood 45, 46

Lawton, Thomas 48
Leasowe Crossing 91, 92
Lee Road 27
Leslie, Major 83
Lever, Lord 76
Linaker, Nellie 65, 66
Livingstone Street 39, 40
Lonnie, Charles 100
Lonnie, Mrs 101
Lydia Terrace 109, 110

Mackenzie, Dr 33
Maddock Street 109, 110
Market Street 13, 14
McFarlane, Susan 124
McGuinness, Bella 10, 11
McHale, Superintendent 37
McKeller, Harold 47, 48
McKeller, Walter 47, 48, 49
McLennon, Valentine 82
McNarney, Mr 90
McNeil, Inspector 89
McNier, Mr 115
Meadow Lane 80
Mersey Road 21, 22
Mill, Dr 61
Mill Street 29
M'Lay, Mr 119
M'Lay, Mrs 119
Moon, Mr 65
Moore, Mr 35
Mortimer Street 53, 54
Muir, Dr 94

Nesbitt, John 47
New Chester Road 54, 108
Newington, Dr 69
Nightingale, George 32, 33
Noble, Dr 84, 85
North Street 17

Oak Street 89
Ockleston, Mary 67, 68, 69
O'Gara, Private 74
Old Chester Road 107
Ostle, Mr 26
Oval, The 71, 72
Owens, John 91

INDEX

Pacific Hotel 120, 121
Park Way 99
Parker, Superintendent 49
Parkings, Frederick 98
Pearson, Dr 22
Pickford, Private 74
Pleavin, Ellen 32, 33
Pleavin, Frankie 32, 33
Pleavin, James 33
Plevin, Joseph 86, 88
Plough Inn 91
Plummer, Professor 74
Pool Street 104, 106
Poole, Joseph 21, 22
Preece, Dr 49
Preston, Mr 110
Price, PC 117
Price Street 120
Priory Street 47, 49

Queens Arms Hotel 88
Queens Hotel 109, 121

Rainford, Mrs 20
Rainford, William 20
Ramsey, William 64
Ranelagh Hotel 117
Reed's Lane 91
Reinhardt, Mr 123
Richardson, Mr 52, 53
Ricketts, Dr 30, 31
Ridgeway, David 92
Rimmer, Elizabeth 30, 31
Roberts, John 61
Roberts, Mr 53
Robson, Dr 22
Rock Lane West 62
Rodney Street 93, 94
Rohlederer, John 100
Rowbottom, Arthur 95
Rowbottom, Frank 95, 96
Rowbottom, Maud 95
Rowlands, Judge Bowen 100, 101

Royal Standard Hotel 112
Rudgrave Square 23, 24
Ryan, Dr 31
Ryan, PC 102

Sampson, Mr 125
Sankey, Mrs 25
Scholes, Mrs 57, 58
Scholes, William 57, 58
Seagrave Street 107
Shaw, Samuel 29
Sherlock, Robert 107, 108
Sidney Road 32
Silcock, Madge 27, 28
Slatey Road 61
Smith, Frederick 100
Smith, George 97, 98
Smith, John Howson 124, 125
Smith, Superintendent 53, 54, 55
South Bank 88
Stephenson, PC 32, 33
Stokes, Thomas 34
Stonehouse, Emily 67, 68, 69
Sydney Street 17

Taggart, Thomas 121, 123
Talbot, Edward 101
Taylor, Edward 118
Taylor, Hannah 118
Taylor, Joseph 118
Taylor, Miss 99
Taylor, Mr 18
Temple, Dr 63
Thomas, John 87
Thomas, Mary 63
Thomas, Richard 62, 63
Thompson, Mayor J.T. 77, 78
Thorpe, Dr 99
Tinsley, Private 73, 74
Tobin, Mr A. 100

Tottey, William 28
Traynor, Mrs 41, 42
Turret Road 37

Vaughn, Dr 90
Victoria Hotel 60
Victoria Park 79, 80

Water Street 13
Watson Street 60
Weaver, Thomas 97, 98
West, Dr 61
West Float 64
Whelligan, Thomas 48
Whetstone Lane 71, 119
Whitby, John 96
Whitfield, Street 29
Whittaker, Berry Thomas 65
Wilkinson, Dr 49, 104, 106
Williams, Edith 100
Williams, Ivy 39, 40
Williams, Mary Jane 39, 40
Williams, Mrs 100
Williams, Sergeant Benjamin 82, 83
Willmer Road 50, 118
Wilson, Dr 94
Wilson, Esther 79, 80
Wilson, Henry 79, 80
Wilson, Moses 80
Witham, Charles 80
Woodey, Dr Ernest 112, 113
Worth, Arthur 28
Wright, Mr Justice 123
Wright, PC 64
Wye Street 80
Wyse, Dr 29

Young, Mrs 51